Geckos

Day Geckos • Tokay Geckos
Plus New Caledonians and more!

FROM THE EXPERTS AT
ADVANCED VIVARIUM SYSTEMS™

Edited by Julie Bergman

THE HERPETOCULTURAL LIBRARY™
Advanced Vivarium Systems™
Irvine, California

Karla Austin, Business Operations Manager
Nick Clemente, Special Consultant
Kendra Strey, Project Editor
Honey Winters, Designer
Cover and layout concept by Michael Vincent Capozzi
Indexed by Melody Englund

Front and back cover photos by Paul Freed.
All photos by Paul Freed except where otherwise indicated. The additional
photographs in this book are by © 2006 Jupiterimages Corporation, p. 8;
Gerold Merker (courtesy of Julie Bergman), pp. 9, 29, 52, 61, 65, 75, 81, 85,
149; Zig Leszczynski, pp. 14, 24, 39, 62, 63, 72, 73, 80, 87, 101, 102, 111, 112,
130, 141; Bill Love, pp. 19, 23.

LCCN: 96-183295
ISBN: 1-882770-89-7

An Imprint of BowTie Press®
A Division of BowTie, Inc.
3 Burroughs
Irvine, CA 92618
866-888-5526

Printed and bound in Singapore
10 9 8 7 6 5 4 3 2 1

CONTENTS

ACKNOWLEDGMENTS

This book could not have been written without the talent and generous help of colleagues who were willing to share their great knowledge of geckos with me. First among these is Sean McKeown, whose books *The General Care and Maintenance of Tokay Geckos and Related Species* and *The General Care and Maintenance of Day Geckos* inspired this book and from which the chapters on these two species are drawn. I was first introduced to the herpetological community and Sean McKeown's research on day geckos (*Phelsuma*) through the Northern California Herpetological Society (NCHS) meetings I attended during my college years. When I decided to specialize in the beautiful sticky-fingered day geckos with amazing colors, Sean, then curator of the Chaffee Zoological Gardens in Fresno, California, kindly agreed to mentor me. He continued as my mentor until his untimely death in 2002. His extensive knowledge of herpetology and his enthusiasm for *Phelsuma* species greatly inspired me to write about the subject and share what I learned with the gecko community.

For the present volume, I also owe special thanks to Philippe de Vosjoli, whose expertise (along with that of colleagues Ron Tremper, Roger Klingenberg, and Brian Viets) forms the basis of information on leopard and crested geckos in this book. I appreciate Philippe's leadership in the herpetocultural community, his creation of the lovely *Vivarium* magazine, his numerous outstanding gecko books, and his basic concepts of herpetoculture.

I am grateful to several other major contributors for the vast gecko knowledge base we all enjoy today: to Ron Tremper, for his tremendous knowledge of all things leopard gecko; Tim Tytle, especially for his ground-breaking early work with day geckos; Magnus Forsberg, for his contributions to day gecko knowledge and the online community; Greg and Leann Christenson, for their dedication to *Phelsuma* species and wonderful book on these geckos; Allen Repashy, for his work on New Caledonian geckos (*Rhacodactylus*); Lee Grismer, for his work on leopard geckos and their relatives; Friedrich Wilhelm Henkel and Wolfgang Schmidt, for their extensive work in the field; and Philip Tremper, for his knowledge of just about every gecko you can think of!

Additionally, I wish to thank the staff and students at the University of California—Davis Veterinary School of Medicine and Veterinary Medical Teaching Hospital for an outstanding job providing my extensive gecko collection with medical care and educating me about gecko medical needs for the past twenty years. I cannot thank enough the following veterinarians, past and present, from UC Davis: Lisa Tell, DVM, Diplomat of the American Board of Veterinary Practitioners (ABVP) (Avian Practice) and American College of Zoological Medicine (ACZM); Michelle Hawkins, VMD, Dipl. ABVP (Avian Practice); Shannon Riggs, DVM; Jennifer Graham, DVM; Annaliese Strunk, DVM; and Keith Benson, DVM. Finally, I would like to thank the Global Gecko Association (GGA) for their excellent Internet resources and fine publications; Gerold Merker for his enthusiasm and excellence in photographing my geckos; my show partner, Cyndi Diekmann, for sharing the "gecko madness" with me over the years; and my husband, Peter Bergman, for putting up with it all!

INTRODUCTION

The goal of this book is simple: to provide the reader with a straightforward, practical source of information on selecting and keeping geckos. Many gecko admirers wishing to keep a gecko are lost in the jungle of pet shops, reptile shows, and Web sites, confused as to which gecko is right for them. In my twenty-two years of keeping and breeding geckos, I made a lot of mistakes, mainly due to misinformation or no information at all. I unknowingly bought unhealthy animals, was given wrong advice, and spent long hours with veterinarians trying to fix these mistakes. Back then, successful private breeders (as I would later become) who were willing to share information were rare, and powerful sources of information such as the Internet didn't exist. Thank goodness times have changed!

Our gecko knowledge base has vastly increased since my early days of gecko keeping in the 1980s, and today it's much easier to get correct information and healthy geckos—the two necessary ingredients for successful gecko keeping. Many of you to whom I have introduced geckos have asked me where my gecko book is—here it is! It is my distinct pleasure and honor to serve as your guide to the gecko world. Novice and experienced keepers alike will learn about which species make good choices for their skill levels.

A wide variety of "herp" products are available to you at pet shops and through online suppliers, but for our purposes we will discuss simple, inexpensive gecko housing setups. Keeping geckos involves a relatively small investment of time and money compared with the expense of traditional pets such as cats and dogs, plus there's the added benefit of observing beautiful geckos and their interesting behaviors in the comfort of your home.

In a nutshell, this book will offer you an educated snapshot of the many geckos available as pets today, such as the extremely popular leopard (*Eublepharis macularius*) and crested (*Rhacodactylus ciliatus*) geckos. We'll focus on the most familiar geckos and talk about the many reasons they have fascinated so many reptile keepers. Let the gecko madness begin!

Leopard geckos (*Eublepharis macularius*)—such as this beautiful high-yellow specimen—who do well in the vivarium and are easy to care for, are undoubtedly the geckos most popular with beginners. However, many other species also do very well, and hobbyists with only moderate experience can keep and breed them succcessfully.

CHAPTER 1

WHY ARE GECKOS POPULAR?

Cultural images of geckos abound: these lizards are used in logos and icons in television and print marketing campaigns; their images are printed on clothing and engraved into jewelry; and they are the subjects of abstract art and handicrafts sold in southwestern-themed boutiques.

Geckos are hailed by some cultures and ethnic groups as symbols of good fortune. In Hawaiian culture, for instance, people consider their gecko populations good luck because of their tremendous insect-eating skills.

Gecko images, such as the stylized mosaic one on this decorative planter, are commonly used today and are an indicator of the popularity of these lizards.

So, what makes a gecko a good pet? Consider the following:

- They come in amazing colors and shapes and have interesting behaviors.
- Many species are ideal for small vivarium setups.
- Many species are long lived (leopard geckos often live until their teens!).
- They have no fur or feathers to sneeze at (though a few people are allergic to bits of shed skin).
- Two readily available types—leopard and crested geckos—are well suited for beginning hobbyists.
- Healthy, captive-bred specimens are easily obtained.
- Keeping a gecko in an attractive, well-prepared vivarium brings nature into your home.

This Central American banded gecko (*Coleonyx elegans*) is a eublepharid gecko. Species of the Eublepharidae family, unlike those of the Gekkonidae family (the majority), have eyelids.

Gecko Classification

Geckos are a reptile group of more than one thousand species populating all the major continents except the polar caps. As a result of living in many environments on different continents, geckos have evolved as a diverse group called the Gekkota. Traditionally, geckos and their relatives were placed in two (Gekkonidae and Pygopodidae) or three (Eublepharidae, Gekkonidae, and Pygopodidae) families, but recently some authorities have broken the Gekkonidae into three groups treated as full families: Gekkonidae proper, Diplodactylinae, and Carphodactylidae. Pygopodidae are slender, nearly legless lizards of Australia and New Guinea and are not found in the hobby on a regular basis. Because our focus is on just a few familiar types of geckos and not their detailed taxonomy (the study of the identification and relationships of living things), we will use a simple and familiar classification that recognizes two families, Eublepharidae and Gekkonidae, with several subfamilies in the Gekkonidae. Geckos that currently are available and of interest to hobbyists of all levels are shown in the following chart. Note that there are more geckos in each subfamily than those you see listed here, and some occasionally appear in the hobby.

Family and Subfamily	Familiar Genera	Notes
Eublepharidae	*Coleonyx*, banded geckos	Distribution: United States, Mexico, Central America Habitat: terrestrial species, found in deserts to tropical forests Activity: nocturnal Foods: crickets, mealworms
Eublepharidae	*Eublepharis*, leopard geckos	Distribution: W. India, Pakistan, Afghanistan, Iraq, Iran Habitat: terrestrial species, found in deserts Activity: nocturnal Foods: crickets, mealworms
Gekkonidae, Gekkoninae	*Phelsuma*, day geckos	Distribution: Madagascar and nearby islands; many species Habitat: arboreal species with sticky feet, found in tropical areas Activity: diurnal Foods: crickets; fruit puree and mixes
Gekkonidae, Gekkoninae	*Paroedura*, Madagascan ground geckos	Distribution: Madagascar and nearby islands Habitat: arboreal or terrestrial species with sticky feet, found in tropical areas Activity: nocturnal Food: crickets

Family and Subfamily	Familiar Genera	Notes
Gekkonidae, Gekkoninae	*Uroplatus*, leaf-tailed geckos	Distribution: Madagascar Habitat: arboreal and terrestrial species with sticky feet, found in tropical areas Activity: nocturnal Food: crickets
Gekkonidae, Gekkoninae	*Chondrodactylus*, Namib Desert geckos; *Geckonia*, helmeted geckos; *Pachydactylus*, tiger geckos; *Palmatogecko*, web-footed geckos	Distribution: Africa Habitat: terrestrial species found in deserts Activity: nocturnal Foods: crickets, mealworms
Gekkonidae, Gekkoninae	*Teratolepis*, viper geckos	Distribution: Pakistan and N. India Habitat: terrestrial species Activity: nocturnal Food: crickets
Gekkonidae, Gekkoninae	*Gekko*, tokay geckos and related species	Distribution: southern Asia Habitat: arboreal species with sticky feet, found in tropical areas Activity: nocturnal Foods: crickets; fruit purees and mixes
Gekkonidae, Teratoscincinae	*Teratoscincus*, wonder geckos	Distribution: Middle East to China Habitat: terrestrial species Activity: nocturnal Foods: crickets, mealworms
Gekkonidae, Diplodactylinae	*Rhacodactylus*, New Caledonian geckos	Distribution: New Caledonia Habitat: tropical Activity: nocturnal Foods: crickets; fruit puree and mixes

Gecko Characteristics

As we discussed, geckos live on nearly every continent, and the various gecko species have adapted to life in diverse climates and terrains. Geckos have developed dramatically different physical characteristics (morphology) and behaviors that enable them to thrive in their respective environments. In the following paragraphs we'll discuss some of the ways geckos differ from other lizards yet share some interesting and unique characteristics with them.

Size

The largest living gecko species is the giant New Caledonian gecko (*Rhacodactylus leachianus*), which has a snout-to-vent length (body length) of about 10 inches (25 centimeters) and a total length of roughly 16 inches (41 cm) (EBML database, Internet, 2005). This gecko's tail is short, making the body size even more impressive. One of the smallest gecko species is *Paroedura androyensis*, Grandidier's Madagascar ground gecko, with a total length of just 3¼ inches (8 cm). Even smaller are a few reef geckos (genus *Sphaerodactylus*) from tropical America, as small as 1½ inches (3.8 cm) in total length; these geckos are among the smallest known vertebrate animals. Most gecko species fall within a length range of 3 to 8 inches (7.5 to 20 cm) and may vary quite a bit within a species. The familiar leopard gecko, for example, commonly ranges from 6 to 8 inches (15 to 20 cm), but some may be more than 10 inches (25 cm).

Feet

Geckos have a great variety of specializations in foot shape, size, and function. They either have "sticky" feet developed for an arboreal (tree-dwelling) lifestyle, as does the day geckos (genus *Phelsuma*) from the Madagascan region; or they have "nonsticky" feet, most useful for life on the ground, as does the leopard gecko (*Eublepharis macularius*). The feet of some geckos, such as the wonder geckos, genus *Teratoscincus*, are designed for burrowing and digging. Some geckos have claws; some of them do not. Perhaps the most interesting feet belong to the web-footed

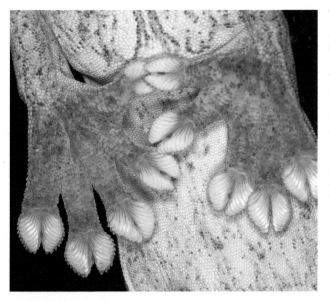

Most geckos are climbers and have toes bearing wide pads at their tips like the ones shown here. The pads are lined with microscopic hairs that allow the lizards to get a grip on minor irregularities and climb smooth-appearing surfaces such as glass.

gecko, *Palmatogecko rangei*. This interesting gecko from the Namib Desert in southwestern Africa uses its webbed feet to run on top of the sand.

Many geckos have a complex toe pad system (called adhesive lamellae) that allows the lizard to run over seemingly smooth surfaces, including glass, without slipping off. Geckos do not have "glue" on their feet to help them run along a surface; rather, some can form the toe pads into tiny suction cups that help them adhere to a surface. As with other lizards with pads under the fingers and toes, the gecko's secret lies mostly in the presence of thousands of microscopic cilia, or hairs, on these pads. These hairs take a variety of shapes that allow the gecko to "hook" into tiny irregularities in the climbing surface and hold on as the other foot steps onto the next part of the surface. This phenomenon is similar to the way Velcro works. Even glass and plastics are not perfectly smooth; they contain microscopic pits and ridges the gecko can use to climb. Because the hairs actually hook into the surface, it is possible for a sleeping or even dead gecko to continue hanging on to a "smooth" surface.

Recent research indicates there may be even more complex scientific explanations for the gecko's ability to run so effortlessly across slippery surfaces, including the use of the actual forces that hold together molecules in the surface—but the idea of "climbing hairs" is hard enough for most keepers to accept.

Eyes

As in many other reptiles, the eyes of a gecko are covered with a fixed plate called a spectacle, or brille, that is shed along with the skin of the head. In the leopard gecko and its relatives (family Eublepharidae), eyelids are present, and a leopard gecko can close its eyes to sleep and to blink. The other geckos (family Gekkonidae) do not have eyelids, so the eyes are always open.

This close-up of the eye of a tokay gecko (*Gekko gecko*) shows the vertical, slitlike pupil typical of most nocturnal geckos. The pupil also displays a pattern of small, round openings that help pinpoint light on specific parts of the retina.

Another major difference in gecko eyes is the type of pupil. Nocturnal (active at night or during low-light conditions) geckos, such as leopard geckos, have slit pupils (similar to a house cat's) that will dilate widely at night, allowing nighttime visual receptors to receive maximum input. Diurnal (day-active) species, such as day geckos, are not as active at night and therefore have round pupils that concentrate light better on the eye's center, which contains the most daytime visual receptors, better equipping these geckos for daylight activity. Small horns or other projections over the eyes of some geckos possibly serve to reduce the glare of bright lights on the eye.

This satanic leaf-tailed gecko (*Uroplatus phantasticus*) is beautifully concealed against the bark by its camouflage pattern of browns, tans, and white. Camouflage is an important means of defense in geckos.

Color and Pattern

As a rule, geckos have colors and patterns that allow them to blend into the background and avoid predators. Desert geckos tend to be shades of yellow and tan, often with bars or blotches on their backs that let them virtually disappear in sandy or pebbly areas. Many tree-dwelling geckos, such as leaf-tailed geckos (genus *Uroplatus*), look like tree bark to camouflage them in their woodsy habitats. Active diurnal tropical geckos, such as the giant day gecko (*Phelsuma madagascariensis grandis*), often are predominantly green and blend in well with lush tropical environments. Day geckos and other brightly colored diurnal geckos are thought to have color vision and may use their different

This white-lined gecko (*Gekko vittatus*) is not suffering from some strange disease. It is an example of a piebald or broken pattern much desired by some keepers.

colors and patterns to help members of the same and different species recognize each other during courtship, preventing interspecies matings.

Scales

Most geckos are covered with hundreds of tiny, pebblelike scales, giving the lizard a soft, velvety appearance. This is one general characteristic of geckos as a group, but of course there are exceptions. For instance, wonder geckos of the genus *Teratoscincus* have large scales they can rattle when disturbed, perhaps to fool a predator into thinking it has disturbed a dangerous snake. At the other extreme, many geckos, such as the crested gecko (*Rhacodactylus ciliatus*), have tiny, soft, virtually indistinguishable scales that look like smooth skin to the naked eye. The leopard gecko (*Eublepharis macularius*), has smooth skin with larger tubercles, or bumps, scattered over the trunk and tail. Most geckos have fairly tough, durable skin that does not tear easily, but others cannot be handled safely because their skin tears easily (*Phelsuma* species) or their scales come off (*Teratoscincus* species).

Shedding

Shedding, or molting of the skin, is a source of great mystery and fascination for gecko owners, old and new alike. Geckos shed frequently when they are young and growing quickly;

When this leopard gecko (*Eublepharis macularius*) finishes shedding, it probably will eat the skin, a normal behavior for most geckos.

shedding occurs less frequently in older geckos. Most geckos eat their shed skin before their human caretakers ever realize they have shed at all. It is quite a shock the first time a new gecko keeper sees his or her gecko with milky white skin— an indicator of a coming shed. Some species, such as the Australian northern velvet gecko (*Oedura castlenaui*), do not eat their skin and simply leave it in the vivarium like a dirty old T-shirt, never to be worn again.

Reproduction

Geckos lay at least one clutch (consisting of two eggs per clutch) during the breeding season, though most species lay several clutches a season. Very few, such as those of the beautiful New Zealand genus *Naultinus*, bear live young. Once gecko eggs are laid, that is the end of the parental relationship in the gecko world, except for a small number of species, such as the popular tokay geckos (*Gekko gecko*), that actually guard their eggs and protect their offspring. Rare parthenogenic geckos, such as the house gecko (*Hemidactylus garnoti*), represent yet another variation in reproduction, having the ability to self-fertilize and produce viable eggs. Gecko eggs are either hard-shelled, as is the case in day gecko (*Phelsuma*) species, or leathery, as in the case of the leopard gecko and other *Eublepharis* species. *Phelsuma* and *Eublepharis* species are also examples of the many gecko species in which higher relative temperatures during incubation produce males, and lower temperatures produce females; this is known as temperature-dependent sex determination (TSD).

Tail Loss

As a defense mechanism, geckos can drop (disconnect) their tails, which, depending on the species, may or may not grow back. Voluntary loss of the tail is known as autotomy. The leopard gecko's tail grows back, but the crested gecko's tail does not. Regenerated tails look different than original tails because they have cartilage in place of bone, giving the tails a different, often almost turniplike, shape; and the full original scalation and coloration seldom

When a gecko, such as this high-yellow morph leopard gecko, loses its tail, it usually regenerates one. However, the new tail may have a different scale pattern and be shorter than the original.

develop. Many geckos, including the leopard and day geckos, use their tail for fat storage; but many others, including the leaf-tailed geckos, do not.

Other Characteristics

Geckos can also hear well and have obvious external ear openings. Most use their thick, slightly notched tongue to lick their eyeballs! Some geckos, such as the leopard and

This baby Madagascan giant day gecko (*Phelsuma madagascariensis grandis*) uses its tongue to clean its eye. Geckos have a thick, fleshy tongue usually notched at the tip.

tokay geckos, have the ability to vocalize, which they do in situations in which they feel threatened and in courtship behaviors.

Sexing

In general, most geckos need to be at least three months old to be large enough for you to determine their sex. The easiest way to do this is to look at the underside of your gecko, either by turning it over gently or by putting it in a clear plastic jar and raising it over your head to view the animal from below (the jar method is recommended for delicate species such as day geckos). Look for the presence or absence of hemipenial bulges (which hold the male sexual organs) behind the vent. Femoral pores in front of the vent are often enlarged in sexually mature males. During breeding season, there is often a visible waxy substance containing gecko pheromones coming out of the male's femoral pores. Males mark their territory with these pheromones that both males and females of the same species will recognize.

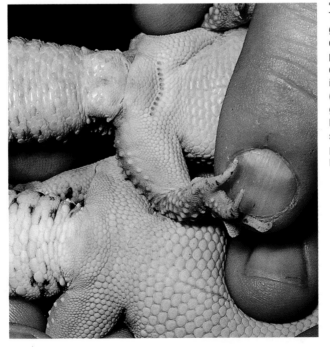

The male leopard gecko here (top) has distinct brownish pores that are absent or poorly developed in the female (bottom). Males generally have the base of the tail swollen by obvious pouches for the hemipenes.

Gecko Behaviors

All geckos are cold-blooded, meaning they cannot regulate their own temperatures and thus rely on warmth from their environments to metabolize food and carry out bodily functions. A gecko achieves the correct temperature by thermoregulating, that is, moving to a warm spot to get warm and moving away when it needs to cool off. (See chapter 3 for information on heating and lighting and how to set up your lizard's cage to provide the opportunity for your pet to thermoregulate.)

Geckos show their best and brightest colors when they are active. Diurnal geckos are most active during daylight hours and when the gecko is optimally warm. Nocturnal geckos are not as dependent on heat as their diurnal counterparts and are most active during night hours. However, both diurnal and nocturnal geckos are not active solely during the day or at night; rather, they usually exhibit varying degrees of activity during both periods. For example,

This day-old tokay gecko (*Gekko gecko*) can snap at a finger just as quickly as an adult can. Geckos come out of the egg as active miniatures of their parents, ready to run, feed, and defend themselves.

nocturnal leopard geckos are seen foraging for food and basking during the day. Some nocturnal geckos in general will stalk food items during the day if hungry enough. During their active periods, geckos will hunt for food, defend their territories (tail waving, chasing), and mate.

Courtship behavior and territorial behavior are, in many cases, so similar to each other that they are easily mistaken for each other. For example, two leopard geckos waving their tails and chasing each other could be defending their respective territories, or they could be engaged in mating behavior. Experience in keeping geckos and observing these behaviors is the best way for the new keeper to learn and understand exactly what his or her pets are doing.

If threatened, geckos prefer to escape and hide; if they cannot hide, they may jump and hiss (especially eublepharid geckos, such as the leopard and the banded). Another alternative is biting; any gecko more than 4 inches (10 cm) long can inflict a bite you will notice. This is how many novice keepers discover their geckos have teeth! If a gecko cannot avoid stress (for instance, if continuously exposed to a stressor such as an aggressive cage mate), it will show dark stress coloration. If the stressor is not removed, the gecko eventually will stop any normal behavior (such as eating) and die. Healthy geckos show good color, whereas ill or stressed geckos do not.

CHAPTER 2

SELECTION

B efore deciding to purchase a gecko, the buyer needs to determine if he or she is ready to commit to a gecko as a pet. This means feeding insects such as crickets and mealworms to the gecko on a regular basis (about three to four times weekly for most adult geckos), seeing to the gecko's watering needs (some species need a water dish, others need their vivarium to be misted daily), keeping the gecko in a quiet area protected from predators such as a cat, providing it with a specific environment, and being prepared to go to (and pay for!) a veterinarian who has special training in reptiles and amphibians if the gecko shows signs of illness. Many species are quite long-lived (leopard geckos can live well into their teens), so a long-term commitment is necessary. If willing to make this commitment, aspiring gecko keepers as young as eight years old (with a little support from adults) can be completely responsible for the easiest of all species, the leopard gecko (*Eublepharis macularius*).

Namib sand geckos (*Palmatogecko rangei*), such as the one shown here, are delicate and require unusual vivarium conditions to be perfectly happy. Such a species would be better suited for an experienced keeper.

Selecting the Right Species

You have been captivated by geckos—their stunning colors, the bright reds and deep blues of tokay geckos (*Gekko gecko*); the soft skin of crested geckos (*Rhacodactylus ciliatus*); the sheer size and weight of the giant New Caledonian gecko (*R. leachianus*); the tiny size of the viper gecko (*Teratolepis fasciata*); the awesome bug-eating power of the large-jawed lined leaf-tail (*Uroplatus lineatus*); and the Zen-like peacefulness of the leopard gecko (*Eublepharis macularius*). How can you possibly decide? Let's start by determining your experience level with geckos and other reptiles and amphibians.

No Experience (Novice)

If you're new to the reptile world, your best bet is the leopard gecko *(Eublepharis macularius)* or the crested gecko (*Rhacodactylus ciliatus*), in that order. The leopard gecko is by far one of the easiest and hardiest reptiles in the pet trade. Creating a simple desert-type vivarium required for keeping this long-lived lizard is easy for beginners to master. Gecko keepers of all experience levels love the fascinating crested gecko because it's easy to keep, too. But this tropical species needs misting daily—a commitment novices may not want to make—and its vivarium is a bit more complex than that of the easier-to-keep leopard gecko (see Chapter 10 for details).

Bred for generations in captivity, leopard geckos such as this one are hardy, feed well, and are happy in a simple vivarium. A beginner can keep and learn from this type of gecko before moving on to a more demanding species.

Reptile Experience, But No Gecko Experience

This type of novice already understands the basic functions and needs of reptiles and amphibians and is familiar with setting up vivaria. Amphibian and chameleon keepers usually grasp the concepts of keeping geckos quickly because they already have mastered the care of their charges, which is usually more demanding and complex than that of geckos. The geckos recommended for this experience level are many and will be noted by species in Chapters 6–11. Some popular choices are: two large, hardy day geckos—the giant day gecko (*Phelsuma madagascariensis grandis*) and Standing's day gecko (*P. standingi*); the viper gecko (*Teratolepis fasciata*); and a beautiful species from New Caledonia, the gargoyle gecko.

In recent years, gargoyle geckos (*Rhacodactylus auriculatus*) have proven to be easy to keep and breed in captivity and can be a good selection if you already have some experience with keeping lizards.

Experienced Gecko Keepers

After mastering the easy-to-care-for species, a keeper with intermediate-level knowledge may want to graduate to more challenging geckos from different genera and, eventually, different families. For your first specimen in "unfamiliar territory," I recommend choosing the hardiest species of the genus you want to explore. Soon, the intermediate keeper can move on to additional species within the genus, each acquisition having increasingly more difficult care requirements. It is important to stick with a genus until you have a thorough understanding of the group's needs. Additionally,

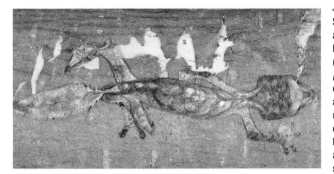

Some geckos, such as this satanic leaf-tailed specimen (*Uroplatus phantasticus*), are delicate, need lots of attention, and require much terrarium experience from the keeper. Only advanced hobbyists should keep one.

the gecko keeper should avoid overloading himself or herself with too many different types of geckos; this is called acquisition fever and often results in losses and frustration of the keeper.

Advanced gecko keepers have been keeping geckos for many years, particularly more difficult members of a genus, such as the satanic leaf-tailed gecko (*Uroplatus phantasticus*). Usually, a short consultation with the breeder of a gecko of interest will provide enough information for an advanced keeper to decide whether he or she would like to acquire a certain species.

Selecting a Healthy Gecko

There are several things to remember when shopping for the gecko of your dreams. First, is the gecko healthy? Captive-bred geckos should be your first choice because they are less likely to have health problems than wild-caught geckos. If shopping at a pet store, check to see if healthy geckos are kept in the same cage with sick reptiles. If so, look elsewhere—the healthy-appearing ones may be sick, too. You do not want to start out your gecko-keeping experience with an unhealthy gecko; it is much more expensive in terms of time, energy, and vet bills than most people realize. The following are considerations in selecting a healthy gecko.

Alertness

A healthy gecko is alert and responsive to stimulation. For example, the gecko should respond to handling by looking at you and moving with vigor. Eyes should be bright, clear, and focused on the stimulation. Geckos with sunken eyes are close to death, so don't buy them.

Appropriate Weight

A healthy gecko shows good weight—be sure you can recognize what your selected gecko species is supposed to look like before you start shopping! Signs of an underweight gecko include a skinny body, a thin tail (in species that store fat in their tail), and protruding hips.

Body Condition

A healthy gecko has good bone structure. Warped jaws, kinked backs, and severely kinked tails are often signs of metabolic bone disease and should be avoided. Slight tail kinks are OK; these are likely consequences of inbreeding and do not affect the health of the gecko. Regenerated tails also are OK; don't rule out that stumpy-tailed gecko! Even a tailless gecko can be a good candidate for a pet because most geckos regenerate new tails or live happily without them. Keep in mind that a gecko with a recent tail loss requires extra attention to nutrition and health during the tail regeneration process.

Skin

A healthy gecko has good-looking skin, free from defects and excessively dark stress coloration. Gecko skin should be without tears, wrinkles (caused by dehydration), or an incomplete skin shed (sign of possible illness). If shopping on the Internet, ask for a photo if there is not one posted online. Some species are difficult to photograph (for example, day geckos are so quick it's hard to catch them); in that case, ask for a thorough description of the gecko.

Other Purchase Considerations

Be sure to get the gecko's correct scientific name, which is necessary in order to get proper care information. Unfortunately, some sellers who know nothing about geckos will not know the scientific name and even make up common names for them such as "big-headed gecko," which is often used for the Madagascan ground gecko, *Pareodura picta*. And if sellers don't know the proper scientific name, how can they provide the correct information for your gecko's proper care? A reputable breeder will accurately identify the species and provide, or at least recommend, care sheets and/or relevant care books.

Ask also about health guarantees; most breeders and pet shops have a policy in place to help you get another gecko or a store credit if your gecko becomes ill or dies shortly after purchase, providing that you followed care instructions properly. From breeders selling geckos on the Internet, ask for guaranteed live arrival; good breeders will give this guarantee. It never hurts to ask for a breeder's references either— it's an advantage to work with a well-known breeder who has been around awhile!

Handling

Handling is an important subject to understand before choosing a gecko. Some geckos can be handled; some should not be handled. The leopard gecko makes a great pet for children because it is one of the easiest to handle, though children should be supervised when handling geckos until they can show they've mastered this skill without hurting or scaring their new reptile friends. Other popular gecko species that can be handled are the crested (*Rhacodactylus ciliatus*), viper (*Teratolepis fasciata*), helmeted (*Geckonia chazaliae*), and fat-tailed (*Hemitheconyx caudicinctus*) geckos.

Many beautiful geckos should not be handled for different reasons: day geckos and frog-eyed geckos (genus *Teratoscincus*) have skin that is easily damaged; other species simply do not like handling. Some of the more popular species that shouldn't be handled are the Madagascan ground (*Paroedura picta*), Central American banded (*Coleonyx mitratus*), and tiger (*Pachydactylus tigrinus*) geckos.

As the gecko keeper gains experience, handling becomes less important. Rather, what makes geckos interesting is seeing them exhibit interesting behaviors in the beautiful vivarium you have created for them.

CHAPTER 3

HOUSING

For geckos to live long and healthy lives, some basic needs must be met. The better you address these needs, the more behaviors and beautiful colors you will see from your gecko. If a gecko is continuously stressed, it usually will stop normal behaviors (such as eating) and eventually die. A common cause of stress is inadequate husbandry practices. Being aware of and providing for your pet's housing requirements are the first steps down the path of responsible reptile care.

The Cage

Typical gecko vivaria are made of glass or a glass-and-screen combination. Glass vivaria are reasonably affordable, easy to clean, and help retain humidity better than all-screen setups do. Specialty stores offer different options to house geckos, including vivaria made of plastic, different composite materials, and Plexiglas, all of which can be attractive and functional in your home.

The size and type of vivarium needed depend on the species of gecko you choose and will be discussed in detail in Chapters 6–11. Generally, though, terrestrial (ground-dwelling) species, such as the popular leopard gecko, will use horizontally oriented setups, whereas arboreal (tree-dwelling) species, such as day geckos, will use vertically oriented setups. Avoid very large glass vivaria (50 gallons, 190 liters, or more) as they will be hard to clean, and geckos may have to work too hard to find their food.

There are different options for vivarium construction; useful options include built-in sliding screen tops. Sliding tops are great for both arboreal and terrestrial vivaria as they provide an access point for the keeper and a good place to put a basking lamp. For a tall, arboreal setup, such as those

A screened area has been cut into the side of this 10-gallon tall vivarium to allow for air movement. Such a vivarium is great for day geckos and other small arboreal species.

for day and New Caledonian geckos, sliding screen doors on one or two sides of the vivarium are convenient. These side doors provide easy access to the cage for you and lessen the risk of escape for the lizard (most geckos prefer to run to the top of the cage). Vivaria may be purchased locally at pet stores and specialty stores, on the Internet, or through ads in reptile magazines.

Vivarium Versus Terrarium

A reptile cage is more formally called a vivarium (plural, vivaria or sometimes vivariums). In this book I'll use the term *vivarium* for any container for a gecko that is not an aquarium—that is for any container with mostly land area, rather than water. In the United States, the term *terrarium* is also used; both vivarium and terrarium are correct. Depending on where you live, one term may be more popular than the other. Both have their advocates; as is so often the case, personal choice determines which one is used. In this book, we use vivarium.

Substrates

The first thing to put in your gecko's new vivarium is what goes on the bottom, the litter or substrate. Which material you use depends on the type of gecko you are keeping.

Pet shops typically offer pre-cut "cage carpet" for popular sizes of leopard gecko vivaria, in addition to more naturalistic options such as fine-grade sand, which usually comes in a nice red color. Coarse grades of sand, which should be avoided due to the tendency of leopard geckos to ingest substrate, which in worst cases results in impaction, a blockage of the gecko's intestinal tract. Most desert dwellers, such as the viper gecko, do well on common play box sand you can purchase from home improvement stores. Do not use construction sand, however, which has sharper edges and could be contaminated with chemicals. Other substrates to be avoided are: fine wood chips, wood shavings, and gravel. Wood chips and shavings are often toxic and can be ingested by the gecko. Gravel, too, poses the risk of possible ingestion when used as the main substrate, but it can be used underneath moss or planting mulch to create drainage routes for plants.

Good, low-budget alternative substrates are paper towels and newspaper, which can be replaced quickly and easily when soiled. Novice gecko keepers should keep their

The green cage carpet in this vivarium makes for easy cleaning and replacement. The tank also has a sliding screen top that provides easy access and good ventilation.

vivarium substrate simple and easy to clean while they are learning about their gecko's husbandry regimen and habits.

Tropical geckos need substrates that maintain humidity. However, most tropical arboreal geckos, such as the giant day gecko, do not spend much time on the substrate, so a flooring of about 2 to 3 inches (5 to 7.5 cm) of sphagnum moss covered with orchid bark will do nicely. Orchid bark comes in fine, medium, and large grades; the type used depends on the size of the gecko or, more precisely, the size of the gecko's mouth. When selecting orchid bark, look at the gecko's head size and try to match it with the bark size to avoid ingestion of the substrate. For instance, a large arboreal gecko, such as Henkel's leaf-tailed gecko (*Uroplatus henkeli*), typically picks up a lot of substrate while devouring a food item, such as a tasty cricket, so large-grade orchid bark should be used to keep smaller bits from being ingested. Generally, geckos are good at spitting out orchid bark and ingesting only the cricket, provided there is not much bark to spit out.

Many tropical terrestrial geckos, such as the Central American banded (*Coleonyx mitratus*) and the Madagascan ground (*Paroedura picta*) geckos do well on a 70 percent play-sand to sphagnum-moss mix. This mixture provides them with the humidity they need to be comfortable and shed properly.

A common mix for tropical gecko substrate includes orchid bark of the proper size for the species, some sand, sterile loam, and perhaps some sphagnum moss.

Cage Decorations

A properly set up vivarium addresses the needs of the occupants just as a furnished house does for humans. Geckos need things to sit on and to hide in. Plants and bamboo work well for arboreal tropical geckos. Plants should accomplish two functions: provide places to sit and places to hide. Here's a short list of sturdy plants to consider:

- *Aglaonema* (Chinese evergreens): these plants look great in large vivaria.
- *Bromeliaceae* (Bromeliads): these are very tropical, exotic-looking plants that look great in large vivaria.
- Crotons (*Codiaeum variegatum*): these are relatively sturdy and colorful tropical plants.
- *Draceana*: the broad leaves provide great retreats.
- Fake plants: you can't kill them!
- Orchids: avoid these delicate beauties if you are not good with plants.
- *Philodendrons*: these are great plants for small geckos to sit on, with large leaves for hiding.
- *Sansevieria* (snake plant or mother-in-law's tongue): these plants tolerate the heat from basking lamps and make great hiding places and egg-laying repositories.

Bamboo is a nice, naturalistic addition to the tropical vivarium and provides places for the gecko to sit and hide. The bamboo pieces should be slightly larger in diameter than your gecko. If bamboo is not available, PVC pipe (white, hollow plastic tubing) is readily available at any home improvement store. At minimum, place a single piece diagonally; preferably, include one horizontally as well. The diagonal and horizontal placement of bamboo will provide the gecko with enough support to avoid an irreversible condition called flap tail (or flop tail), a deformity in which the tail bends backward at a sharp angle. This deformity is thought to be caused by a lack of adequate resting places. I have seen this condition in day geckos, most notably the larger species such as Standing's and giants and the crested and gargoyle (*Rhacodactylus auriculatus*) New Caledonian geckos.

Terrestrial geckos need natural or simulated caves in which they can hide and feel secure. Most pet stores carry a variety of styles of hide boxes. Plastic hide boxes are better than those made out of wood or other porous material because they are easily cleaned and sterilized and thus are reusable. Or, round up some cardboard toilet-paper or paper-towel rolls, which can be disposed of when soiled and easily replaced—and, they're free! Rocks may also be used as caves provided they are glued or wedged together sufficiently to avoid their collapsing on the gecko. Ground-dwelling geckos appreciate driftwood and cholla cactus to walk on and cork bark to hide under (which enables them to get heat without bright light in their sensitive eyes). Additionally, a piece of driftwood or rocks placed strategically will give geckos a desirable place to survey their surroundings in order to hunt for food, display themselves for their mates, or bask. Succulents without large thorns (thick-leaved, water-storing plants such as aloes) and fake plants also look nice in terrestrial vivaria. Place one hiding spot at the warm end of the vivarium and another shelter at the cool end (see also the following discussion on heating and creating a thermal gradient).

In this naturalistic leopard gecko vivarium produced by Vivarium Research Group, the plants include a small fig (*Ficus benjamina*), a snake plant (*Sansevieria*), and a miniature or pony-tail palm, all of which can survive in low-light conditions.

Dishes

There are many beautiful faux-rock water dishes available in the pet trade. These work well because they can be thoroughly sterilized, and their rough surfaces allow live food items to climb out if they accidentally fall in. (A water dish full of dead, stinky crickets is not pleasant!) Choose a water dish shallow and low enough to the ground so your terrestrial gecko can see and get to the water, but make sure it is large enough so the water does not evaporate in just two or three days. Monitor the water dish daily; fill and clean it as needed. Clean the water dish immediately if you see feces in the water, as the fouled water is probably swarming with bacteria. You may also use lids from bottles and jars as water dishes; these are easy to throw away and replace if desired. Many tropical geckos (day geckos, for instance) prefer to drink water droplets off plants. Nonetheless, a water dish is a good idea, and most geckos will drink out of them.

Food dishes are useful for any gecko. Food items such as mealworms are simply put in the dish, which can be a food jar lid or a fancy ceramic dish. A soda bottle cap is an inexpensive option often used to hold fruit-based mixes typically fed to day geckos. As with the water container, the food dish should not be so tall that the gecko cannot easily see the food items, yet tall enough to keep mealworms contained. A shallow food dish won't contain live crickets for long, but it will hold them long enough to give the gecko time to spot the prey and move in for the kill. Vitamin supplements used to coat crickets (see the supplementation section in chapter 4) will tend to fall into the dish, helping to keep the vivarium tidy.

A small dish will hold powdered calcium supplement, which is necessary for breeding females. With the supplement left in the dish placed atop the substrate, the females will wander up and consume the amount of calcium they need.

Heating and Lighting

Providing a heat source for your gecko can be accomplished in a number of ways. Generally, there are preferred methods for each type of gecko.

Terrestrial geckos commonly are heated with an incandescent light, such as a regular household lightbulb or a specialty reptile bulb from the pet shop. Vivaria also can be heated using undertank heaters (UTHs), which are thin plastic pads containing heating elements. Using infrared lamps, which provide heat without visible light, is efficient for nocturnal geckos, which could be bothered by the light. Often a combination of incandescent light and UTH (especially popular in colder climates) is used.

Arboreal geckos also are commonly heated with incandescent lights. The sticky feet of these tree-dwelling species are too easily burned by UTHs, so their use is not recommended. Since many arboreal geckos are diurnal, their vivaria should also be lighted with either fluorescent or full-spectrum lighting for brightness.

Some breeders maintain that a full-spectrum fluorescent lamp that produces both ultraviolet A and ultraviolet B wavelengths (UV-A and UV-B) should be used, maintaining that UV-B is essential for allowing a diurnal gecko to convert calcium into bone. Other breeders believe incandescent light will suffice so long as the animal receives a properly supplemented diet to facilitate calcium absorption. Commonly, a combination of an incandescent lamp (for heat) and a fluorescent tube (for light) is used.

The particular light and heat sources that a species and its relatives require is discussed in Chapters 6–11.

If you are keeping diurnal geckos, such as day geckos (genus *Phelsuma*), it is said to be advantageous for their health and appearance to use a full-spectrum lamp that provides both UV-A and UV-B wavelengths.

Thermal Gradient

To accomplish proper heating you need to know the optimal temperature range that your gecko likes to be in. Typically, a warm area (usually including the basking site) is set up on one side of the cage and maintained at the high end of the temperature range, while the opposite end of the cage is maintained at the low end of the range. The temperature range, formally called a thermal gradient, is vital to your gecko's health. Geckos—(all reptiles for that matter)—must thermoregulate (move to the location that has the desired temperature) to facilitate bodily functions such as digestion and egg development. If not allowed to do this, your gecko will inevitably become ill.

Measuring Temperature

The proper way to check temperatures in your gecko's vivarium is with an accurate temperature measurement device such as a mercury-type thermometer, infrared temperature gun (now available inexpensively), or a high-quality digital temperature probe. Stick-on temperature tapes (LCD thermometers) are not very precise, but they can verify that one end of the vivarium is warmer than the other. In the case of terrestrial geckos, be sure to place temperature tapes as close to the substrate level as possible on both ends of the vivarium. For arboreal geckos, temperature tapes should be located as close to the basking spot as possible (typically up high).

Initial Setup

Before you bring your gecko home, you need to set up its home. This includes establishing the proper thermal gradient specific to the species you keep. Check temperatures during different times of the day to make sure maximum and minimum temperatures are not exceeded, and to be sure your selected temperature-sensing devices are working properly.

Sometimes UTHs develop hot spots that can burn the gecko. For this reason, only UTHs specially made for reptiles should be used and human heating pads avoided. UTHs should also have an adjustable thermostat so temperatures can be raised or lowered as necessary.

Photoperiod

The length of time your gecko is exposed to light each day is called the photoperiod. In vivaria using overhead lighting, lamps should be turned on at sunrise and off at sunset. The easiest way to do this is by setting up lights on automatic timers (another home-improvement store item). If you would like to better observe your gecko in the dark, a low-wattage (25 watts or fewer) red or blue incandescent bulb may be used and won't disturb the animal.

CHAPTER 4

FEEDING

O nce you have your gecko's vivarium set up, your next step is to address its nutritional needs. First, you need to find out from the seller what your new pet's current feeding regimen is—that is, what, when, and how often it eats. This important information is usually provided in a care sheet that comes with the gecko. You must keep your gecko on the same feeding regimen it was on before you obtained it to assure a smooth acclimation to its new home.

Most geckos eat:

- Crickets: They are highly nutritious for geckos and are taken by most species. Crickets should be 90 to 95 percent of the gecko's head width.
- Mealworms: These are larvae of a beetle. As in all wormlike foods, they should be smaller in diameter than the gecko's head width. Mealworm heads do not need to be cut off—it is a myth that they will eat through the stomachs of small, delicate geckos.
- Giant mealworms: They are a cultivated variety of the regular mealworm, fed on hormones to increase size.
- Superworms: They are larvae of a very large, tropical beetle.
- Wax worms: These worms are the larval stage of the wax moth, a brownish moth that lives in beehives. They are high in fat content and should be used only as a snack (highly addictive).
- Cockroaches: These are favorites of leaf-tailed geckos. Use only cultivated forms, not household roaches, which might have been exposed to poisons.
- Flightless fruit flies: They can serve as snack food for small arboreal geckos and as main food for hatchlings.

- Nectar, fruit puree, and commercial foods for tropical geckos: These are used to supplement the diet of day geckos.
- Freeze-dried insects (crickets, fruit flies, mealworms): They can be used if you run out of live food, but they are not substitutes; most geckos will not recognize dead animals as food.

These foods are all conveniently available on the Internet or at pet shops. Commercial insect food has the bonus of being pesticide-free.

This peacock day gecko (*Phelsuma quadriocellata*) eats a sugar-rich supplement. In addition to commercially available products, day geckos will eat drops of nectar, fruit juices, and honey.

Gut-Loading

When you purchase a living food insect, assume it has had nothing to eat and has little nutritional value. You must provide a "gut load" for your food items before they can be fed to your gecko, preferably during a twenty-four-hour period before feeding. A combination of commercial gut-loading formulas, such as the T-Rex Insect Loading Formula and leftover salad greens, works well. Vegetables, such as grated or sliced carrots and potatoes, or orange slices are ideal sources of water for your feeder insects; insects commonly climb into water dishes and drown. Be sure to keep feeder insects in a smooth-sided container tall enough to keep them from escaping. Commercial plastic or glass reptile vivaria accomplish this purpose for mealworms, but crickets will climb plastic. Put pieces of egg cartons in the cage for your feeder insects to have a place to sit and hide. Each type of feeder insect will have specific care and setup needs, so be sure to get a care sheet from the pet shop or mail-order insect dealer.

Mother Nature's Food

If you catch wild insect foods for your gecko, make sure they have not been exposed to pesticides and are soft-bodied (squishy) insects that will easily fit into your gecko's mouth. Hard-bodied insects such as beetles, with their thick, chitinous exoskeletons, are too difficult for your gecko to digest.

Supplementation

Feeder insects need to be supplemented with vitamins and minerals in order for your gecko to get the best nutrition possible in captivity. In general, geckos need supplements containing a 2:1 calcium-to-phosphorus ratio and a 2:1 vitamin D_3–to–vitamin A ratio. Good supplements are available commercially; choose the one recommended by your gecko's breeder for your particular gecko. Coat your gecko's insect food with this supplement right before feeding. The easiest way to do this is to put the food items in a tall plastic cup and sprinkle the supplement on them (a method widely referred to as dusting). Females should have

These crickets have been dusted with calcium powder, which they transfer to the geckos that eat them. Calcium supplements with added vitamins are especially important for young geckos.

access to a dish of calcium powder due to the increased demands on their bodies for eggshell formation when they are sexually mature.

Feeding Schedule

How often your gecko eats depends on how big and how old it is. Young geckos need to eat more frequently than older geckos because they need more energy for growing. When geckos reach sexual maturity (seven to nine months, on average), most of their growth is completed, and their need for food decreases. Many novice gecko owners panic at this time of their gecko's life because they mistake their sexually mature gecko's normal appetite decrease as a hunger strike having to do with illness. Adult gecko appetites also decrease in winter due to cooler temperatures, which slow down their metabolism. Juvenile and hatchling geckos do not experience much of a decreased appetite in winter because they are still growing at that time. It is important to be aware of your gecko's appetite changes because decreased appetite may be a sign of illness, especially if the gecko loses weight and has not eaten for two weeks or more. In this case, obtain trained veterinary help immediately.

As a rule, feed your gecko as many insects as it can eat in about twenty minutes. Remove any uneaten insects; uneaten prey has nothing to eat in the vivarium and thus loses nutritional value. These living leftovers could also possibly attack and overwhelm your gecko.

CHAPTER 5

KEEPING GECKOS HEALTHY

Your new gecko has arrived—congratulations! You are on your way to a long, rewarding relationship. However, there are certain steps you need to take to ensure your new friend adapts to its new surroundings and stays healthy. The importance of proper vivarium setup (correct temperatures, adequate hiding places), nutrition (appropriate food and care regimen), and cleanliness cannot be stressed enough as being critical to keeping your gecko healthy.

Most geckos are long lived and deserving of veterinary treatment when necessary. Geckos can be quite delicate little lizards, and they have their share of parasites and diseases, so it is a good idea to make sure you know of a veterinarian in the area who is trained to handle the problems of reptiles. You also will find that you cannot just bring your gecko home and put it into its vivarium and expect it to start eating and behaving normally. It should go through a process of acclimation and sometimes quarantine.

Acclimation

Acclimation is the process of slowly allowing your gecko to get used to its new home, new foods, and new owner. The best way to make sure acclimation goes smoothly is to have already reviewed a care sheet or appropriate book describing the setup and care of the gecko before you bring the animal home. You must know how the gecko was kept (food type, feeding regimen, vivarium setup) before you bought it so you can duplicate those conditions—this is key

The swelling on the throat and upper chest of this Namib giant ground gecko (*Chondrodactylus angulifer*) is an endolymphatic sac, where many types of female geckos store calcium. The use of this calcium is thought to help produce stronger eggshells.

to the acclimation process. If you cannot get this information from the seller, then do not purchase the gecko.

Ask the Breeder

Before you take your new pet gecko home, be sure to obtain information from the seller about the gecko's current care regime. Abruptly changing the animal's housing and feeding routine can cause stress, making the gecko more susceptible to sickness and even death. Below are some suggested questions that a responsible breeder or pet store salesperson should be able to answer:

- What types of foods is the gecko used to?
- How often does it eat and at what time of day?
- What temperature range is it comfortable in?
- What kind of vivarium setup should I provide for this gecko?
- Is this gecko captive-bred or wild-caught?
- What literature or care sheets are available for this species?

Normally, there is a transition period for the gecko of a few days or even a week or so (with larger specimens) before they eat regularly and start exhibiting normal behavior. This is completely normal, and geckos in good health have adequate fat storage to get them through this adjustment period. During this time, it is important that the gecko be kept in a quiet area, with handling kept to a minimum. Water should always be available, and tropical gecko vivaria should be misted just before the introduction of the gecko.

Mealworms may be offered right away in a dish (if that is what the gecko normally eats), but if crickets are part of the food regimen, they should be introduced the second day and removed after about twenty minutes if not eaten. Uneaten crickets may stress the gecko and make the acclimation period longer.

Once a week or so passes, the gecko may be gradually introduced to handling if it is a species that is the "handling type," such as a leopard gecko (see also chapter 2 and the individual species accounts in Chapters 6–11). In the case of juvenile geckos, avoid handling until they are about three months old.

Let the gecko taste-touch your fingers (much as a dog or a cat does) while it is in the vivarium. Once it is willing to sit on your hand in the vivarium, you may take it out for short periods of time. If it fusses for more than a minute, put it back into the vivarium. Never grab a gecko by its tail— remember that many geckos can voluntarily drop the tail if they feel they are being attacked. Support its whole body with the palm of your hand. If you need to control it, gently squeeze as much of its body as possible with your other hand so no body parts are able to flop around. You may grip the fattest part of a back leg securely without damaging the gecko. (This does not apply to small geckos and those of very slender build or with loose skin.) Be sure to supervise children while they are learning to hold their new pet.

Stress

Much of the stress in keeping geckos comes from trying to keep more than one specimen in a vivarium or by mixing species. No mixing of species should be tried by novice gecko keepers—period! Advanced gecko keepers may consider combinations that are known to work, but it is always best if the combination also occurs in nature, and definitely not as predator and prey. The rules for keeping geckos together are simple:

1. No two males can be kept in the same vivarium, as they will fight, possibly to the death. Many gecko keepers discover they actually had two males that

were thought to be a male-female pair only after one gecko dies of stress. Occasionally a female is not compatible with a male or even other females.

2. Smaller geckos may become food for larger ones, so only geckos of similar size should be put together.

3. Babies should be removed immediately if they happen to hatch out with the parents in the vivarium.

4. Aggressive individuals causing injury to cage mates should be removed immediately. Additionally, if one gecko looks stressed and is not eating well, then isolate that gecko immediately. Stress, with or without contact from another gecko, is a swift and unforgiving killer of geckos.

Overcrowding in general causes stress and injury, frequently in the form of tail-biting. Wounds are also often inflicted during mating. A gecko keeper should worry about wounds in breeding situations if the wounds are behind the shoulders because that usually indicates aggression not related to mating that could seriously hurt the gecko. Mating wounds are typically in front of the shoulders and usually heal fine without intervention. Wide-spectrum antibiotic salves intended for humans may be applied to wounds on gecko skin. Tail stumps from lost tails need no special treatment and heal fine on their own. Stumpy-tailed species, in the case of fat-storing geckos such as leopards, will no longer have fat reserves, so special attention should be paid to their nutrition during the healing and regrowth process. Any large wounds or wounds that are not healing should be treated by a veterinarian with reptile experience.

Quarantine

If you intend to introduce your new gecko to others you already have established in a vivarium, a quarantine of six to eight weeks is recommended. A new gecko needs to be quarantined for health reasons so you can be sure it does not pass diseases to your other geckos. Ideally, the enclosure used for the quarantine period should be kept in a room separate from the room your other geckos reside in. To reduce the risk of cross-contamination, tend to your estab-

Quarantine vivaria are kept as simple as possible so they are easy to clean. Everything in the vivarium should be disposable or sterilizable.

lished geckos first, before you even go near the quarantined gecko. It is imperative that you thoroughly wash your hands after touching your quarantined pet and anything that it touches, such as its cage and cage decorations. The quarantine vivarium should have its own set of dishes and cleaning utensils that never go near the vivaria of your established geckos—don't even wash these items in the same sink. Do not "recycle" uneaten food items from vivarium to vivarium. Live prey may have stepped in gecko feces and spread parasite eggs between cages. Even fruit and other nonliving food items can harbor parasites—anything a sick gecko has touched is possibly contaminated.

The quarantine vivarium should be set up with throw-away hide boxes and paper-towel rolls for basking spots. Paper towels or newspaper should be used as substrate so feces can be monitored closely and removed. Normal feces have a firm, brown center part and a whitish outer part that has a more liquid texture (urine). Ill geckos have consistently abnormal feces that may be green, runny, or foul-smelling. Pay close attention to the gecko's color. Healthy geckos show vibrant color; sick or stressed geckos are usually darker in appearance. A gecko in quarantine should also be of sufficient weight (no hip bones showing) before being released from quarantine. If six to eight weeks pass and weight, color, shedding, behavior (not eating, lethargic), and feces are still abnormal, continue quarantine and make an appointment with a reptile veterinarian. The veterinarian will usually ask you to bring a fecal sample from your gecko to the first appointment to check for parasites. Most parasite problems are treatable if caught early enough.

Selecting a captive-bred gecko is the first priority for a new gecko owner because these geckos have fewer health problems than their wild-caught counterparts. The new gecko owner needs to be alert to any potential health problems their gecko may be experiencing and to a potential health risk to themselves, such as salmonellosis.

Salmonellosis

Salmonellosis (or salmonella infection) is a zoonosis, a disease transmissible from animals to humans. It is thought that most reptiles, including geckos, carry salmonella bacteria. Most reptiles are usually not adversely affected by salmonella bacteria. However, humans (particularly children, the elderly, or adults with otherwise

Reducing Salmonella Risk

Risk of salmonella infection, which occurs from ingestion of gecko feces, can be greatly reduced if the following steps, recommended by the Association of Reptile and Amphibian Veterinarians, are taken:

- Wash your hands in hot, soapy water after handling reptiles and their equipment.
- Do not place geckos on cooking or bathing surfaces used by humans.
- Do not let geckos roam outside of their cages.
- Do not eat, drink, or smoke while handling geckos or their equipment.
- Do not bathe geckos or wash their equipment in sinks or tubs used by humans. Use a separate plastic basin or container designated for this purpose. Dump water from this receptacle into the toilet, not down sinks or bathtubs where contaminated water will hit the basins and sides and possibly pass infection to food items or body parts that next touch the sink or tub.
- Keep your geckos healthy—healthy geckos are less likely to shed salmonella bacteria.
- Supervise young children handling geckos to ensure that they don't put their hands near their mouths and that they wash their hands after handling the animals.

compromised immune systems) are sometimes susceptible to infections, especially when a large quantity of salmonella bacteria is transmitted. For the average, healthy person, a salmonella infection induces varying degrees of mild, short-term illness with symptoms of diarrhea, fever, and abdominal cramps. Once you understand how to reduce your health risks, you may move on to understanding the health risks to your gecko.

Parasites

Most geckos have some degree of endoparasitic infections (internal parasites) as well as mites (external parasites). Usually, geckos can live with low parasite loads without any resulting health problems for their entire lives. However, if a gecko has high parasite load and is continuously kept under stressful situations—such as being housed with aggressive cage mates, being given an improper diet, or contracting other diseases that "gang up" on the lizard's immune system—the gecko may develop health problems. Symptoms include: weight loss (most prevalent, often visible as a "pencil tail"), consistent loss of appetite, lethargy, abnormal feces including partially or completely undigested food in feces, regurgitated skin shed (typical of cryptosporidium problems), shedding problems, and dark stress coloration. If you notice any of these symptoms, seek the help of a reptile veterinarian immediately.

Internal Parasites

If your gecko seems to have internal parasite-related problems, your veterinarian will most likely ask you for a fecal sample from your gecko. This is because the most common parasites of geckos are found in the digestive tract. They include pinworms (oxyurids), which are most common; coccidia (protozoans that form cysts in the lining of the gut); trichomonads (flagellated protozoans often found in the intestines); and cryptosporidia (another type of protozoan).

If caught early enough, all of these are treatable except cryptosporidia, although there are new treatments on the horizon for cryptosporidia, which occurs almost exclusively in leopard geckos (de Vosjoli, Tremper, and Klingenberg 2005). Leopard geckos with cryptosporidia should be kept in permanent quarantine so other geckos in the home are not infected. Many leopard geckos affected by cryptosporidia can live for years while showing few, if any, symptoms. It is usually another stressor that gives this parasite the upper hand.

Your veterinarian will prescribe oral medication for the treatment of most internal parasites as well as recommend a thorough vivarium cleaning on a regular basis to prevent relapse.

Many gecko keepers unwisely decide to medicate their own geckos without doing fecal examinations to see exactly which parasite—if any—is the problem. This practice exposes the gecko to harsh treatment (yes, medication is rough on geckos) and is often wasted effort on the part of the keeper. The guess is usually wrong, and the gecko has to undergo another round of treatment once a fecal test is performed to correctly determine the cause. Reptile veterinarians should do the diagnostic work and suggest treatment regimens; new treatments are being discovered all the time, and only a veterinarian is qualified to decide which approach is best for your gecko.

External Parasites

Ectoparasites (external parasites) are worth mentioning due to their prevalence on wild-caught geckos. These are usually mites that can be transferred to other geckos kept with or near infested geckos. Some keepers suggest using common transparent cellophane tape to remove them, but the effectiveness of this method is not proven. A reptile veterinarian may prescribe a chemical treatment to eliminate them from your gecko.

Check the Labels

Do not use mite treatments intended for snakes on your gecko. These formulas seem to be to harsh for geckos for undetermined reasons, and using them usually will result in the death of your pet.

Shed Problems

One of the most common problems that result in an infection is bits of shed skin stuck on the feet. Skin accumulates with each passing shed and constricts circulation in the toes, which leads to in an infection or the complete loss of toes. Humidity being too low in the vivarium contributes to the problem by making complete shedding more difficult.

Many terrestrial geckos that experience these symptoms will benefit from a hide box with a moist substrate of moss or vermiculite. Margarine tubs with lids work well for this purpose. Cut a hole in the lid just big enough for the gecko to get in through (the larger the hole, the harder to contain the moist substrate). Check the substrate every few days to make sure it is clean and still moist. (This same setup works well for gravid females, which will often enter the tub to lay their eggs in the moist substrate.) Tropical geckos that have shedding problems around the toes will benefit by increasing the humidity in the vivarium. This may be done by increased misting of the cage, planting plants directly in the substrate (planting requires additional moisture-holding substrate to secure the plants, which increases the overall humidity), or both.

Treating constricted skin on toes is easy if there are not too many layers of skin accumulated. If the bits of shed skin are not easily removed with tweezers (be careful not to tear new skin), soak the gecko's feet in warm, shallow water for five minutes or so and then gently attempt to pull off the skin with tweezers. Warm, wet terrycloth towels may also be used to attempt to remove stuck skin shed on feet and other areas. Be extremely careful removing unshed skin from a gecko's eyes as you may permanently damage its sight. Stubborn eye sheds (the old eye caps may turn opaque) are best removed by a reptile veterinarian.

Gut Impaction

Geckos may ingest vivarium substrate and develop a blockage of their digestive system, which is called gut impaction. The symptoms of this problem include decreased or absent appetite and failure to defecate. If

When geckos such as this young Namib sand gecko (*Palmatogecko rangei*) are kept in dry vivaria, they sometimes suffer from incomplete shedding. Small bits of old skin may adhere to the toes, cutting off circulation. Carefully check the feet of all geckos after a shed.

these symptoms develop, consult a reptile veterinarian immediately! The veterinarian may give an oral medication called metroclopramide to help the gecko pass the blockage or even remove the blockage surgically (de Vosjoli, Tremper, and Klingenberg 2005). This is a dangerous problem that occurs because geckos, particularly leopard geckos, seem to want to "clean themselves out" by ingesting substrate when they are not feeling well. Unfortunately, we cannot supply them with the less harmful substrate they usually ingest from their natural environment, so we must take care to use the recommended substrates and pay close attention to any symptoms that may be related to impaction.

One way to prevent impactions is to never offer moistened food items (such as fruit) directly on the substrate. Even with live prey, a keeper may moisten crickets a bit by misting so the calcium supplement adheres better. Yet, at the same time, the moisture causes bits of substrate to stick to the insects thus increasing the chances of an impaction. Offer moistened food in a container or, if not fast-moving live prey, on a plate.

Hypocalcemia and Metabolic Bone Disease

Hypocalcemia is a calcium deficiency in the blood (and eventually the bones) that can lead to a dangerous condition known as metabolic bone disease. Hypocalcemia results

If not given sufficient calcium and vitamins in its food, a gecko (such as this leopard gecko) could suffer from hypocalcemia or metabolic bone disease. This manifests as weak, swollen joints, deformed legs, teeth loss, and a thickened, rubbery lower jaw.

from inadequate nutrition—usually not enough of or a complete lack of vitamin D_3 supplementation and calcium—or from breeding a gecko too young or an adult gecko that is underweight. Geckos experiencing symptoms of hypocalcemia have obvious deformities such as rubber jaw (distorted mouth), crooked feet, or bowed or kinked spines and tails. Tetany (twitching) and complete or partial paralysis may also occur. If you think your gecko is hypocalcemic, consult a reptile veterinarian for treatment. The veterinarian probably will inject a calcium compound and also prescribe an oral treatment of liquid calcium supplement as well as advise you of the proper vitamin supplementation and feeding regimen for your gecko. The treatment may also consist of adding UV-B lighting, which facilitates metabolism of calcium. All reptiles need a certain level of vitamin D_3 in the blood to correctly metabolize calcium from their food and convert it into bone as well as to maintain the proper flow of electrical signals through the nervous system. The UV-B wavelengths react photochemically with a vitamin precursor in the blood to change it to vitamin D_3, which then directs the metabolism of calcium.

Dystocia

Dystocia (egg-binding) is the inability to lay eggs that have been in the reproductive tract longer than normally occurs. It is thought that dystocia is caused by inadequate nutrition or by breeding a gecko that has not reached the optimal age (specifically, the ideal size). However, I have noted egg-binding in a few leopard geckos that were more than three or four years old and that had not been bred before. (In such cases, it is likely that the pelvis has completely fused, so it can no longer expand to allow an egg to pass.) If you can actually see bulges in the skin (indicating the presence of eggs) of your gecko that have been there for four weeks or more, consult your veterinarian for treatment.

Veterinarians may try a drug called oxytocin to stimulate egg laying. This treatment may be supplemented with a calcium injection to promote muscle contraction, which helps expel the eggs. If this does not work, the veterinarian may have to make a slit in the abdominal skin and then the eggs to aspirate the contents of the eggs, allowing them to collapse and the gecko to pass them. I have had this procedure performed on a leopard gecko by a veterinarian at the University of California–Davis Veterinary Medical Teaching Hospital. The operation was a success, and the gecko went on to be a successful breeder for many years. Often, geckos that survive egg-binding are sterilized to avoid further risks to their health.

Hemipene Prolapse

Male geckos experiencing dehydration or constipation may experience hemipene prolapse, in which one or both of their hemipenes cannot be retracted. This usually occurs when the male is straining to defecate. If this happens, isolate the animal and put him on paper towels. Keep the everted hemipenis moist by applying a water-based lubricant until you can get the gecko to the veterinarian for treatment. Sometimes it is possible for the veterinarian to get the gecko to retract the hemipenis, but sometimes the hemipenis must be amputated. If one hemipenis is left, then it is still possible for the male to breed.

Other Common Gecko Maladies

Keeping a gecko at too cool of a temperature for an extended period of time often leads to suppression of the immune system and subsequent respiratory infections. The most common symptoms are gaping of the mouth and labored expirations. Raise the cage temperature a few degrees, but if symptoms do not subside in a day or so, take the animal to a reptile veterinarian.

CHAPTER 6

LEOPARD GECKOS AND RELATIVES

W hen the geckos are broken into multiple families, those having functional eyelids are always the first to be recognized as different. They form what is usually accepted as a full family, the Eublepharidae—the eyelid geckos, or eublepharids, and the leopard geckos and their close relatives. The family comprises more than twenty species and subspecies placed in the genera *Eublepharis* (India to Middle East), *Hemitheconyx* (Africa), *Holodactylus* (Africa), *Goniurosaurus* (southeastern Asia), and *Coleonyx* (southwestern United States to Central America). Though species from all five genera appear in pet shops on occasion, only a half dozen or so species are actually easy to find and keep.

The leopard gecko (*Eublepharis macularius*) is exceptionally hardy, is easy to handle, and breeds readily in a simple vivarium. It also has a lot of personality.

The largest species of this group of readily available eublepharids are the thick-bodied leopard gecko (*Eublepharis macularius*) and the African fat-tailed (*Hemitheconyx caudicinctus*) gecko, at 6 to 10 inches (15 to 25 centimeters) in length. These two large species store fat in their tails, and males are typically larger than females. Next in size are the banded geckos (genus *Coleonyx*), which are slender and smaller, ranging from about 4 inches (10 cm) in *C. variegatus* to about 6 inches (15 cm) in *C. elegans*. Smaller species of *Coleonyx* sometimes may have larger females than the males. All species in this group are nocturnal and terrestrial (cannot climb glass), possess eyelids, and have slender toes with claws but without widened pads.

Unlike most geckos, hatchling leopard geckos (right) don't closely resemble the adults (left). Hatchlings show blackish bands on yellow that break into smaller spots as the geckos mature.

The docile leopard gecko is a favorite because, in addition to being the easiest to care for, it tolerates handling well. The African fat-tail is also known for docility and tolerates a certain amount of handling, as do *C. brevis* and *C. variegatus* (though their small size and thin skin make handling risky). *C. mitratus* and *C. elegans* do not care to be handled and will let you know they are not happy in the typical eublepharid style of jumping and hissing. If not allowed to retreat, these geckos may bite. They may also spontaneously break off the tail under a condition of threat, so pay attention to their warnings. If you handle these geckos with care, within their comfort zone, you will find them sturdy and pleasant pets.

Leopard geckos are famous for producing brightly colored morphs. In the high-yellow morph (top), the dark spotting of the normal leopard (bottom) is virtually absent, and the entire body is bright yellow.

All eyelid geckos are nocturnal and spend most of the day sleeping in hiding places, often wedged in with cage mates. When food is presented and they are hungry, they will run to eat it day or night, often rattling and waving their tails just before they strike at the food item. At night, they are active and frequently can be seen climbing on low objects in the vivarium. If they escape from their cage at night, look for them with a flashlight (overhead lights will scare them into hiding). The first place to look for them is under the refrigerator, where they can usually be teased out gently with a wire hanger. They prefer hiding under the refrigerator because it is warm under there; they may also be found under other heat-generating appliances and furniture.

Housing

Eyelid geckos are terrestrial, so they are best suited to horizontally oriented vivaria. Glass vivaria are best for creating attractive displays. As a low-budget option, you may use clear or opaque plastic storage containers, with small (quarter-inch, 6-millimeter) air holes drilled into the lids for adequate ventilation.

Start with a glass vivarium of 5 to 10 gallons (19 to 38 liters) capacity for one or two *Coleonyx* specimens or 10 to 20 gallons (38 to 76 L) for one or two leopard or fat-tailed geckos. A lid is necessary; a sliding screen top is easier to use than a fixed screen lid. The lid not only keeps the geckos in

and predators (such as cats) out but also serves as a resting place for the basking light. You can make a lid out of sturdy hardware cloth and use duct tape on the sharp edges.

The substrate of choice depends on the gecko being kept, so see the following individual species accounts for details. Typically, the level of moisture the species prefers determines the substrate.

To heat the vivarium, an incandescent basking light screwed into a metal clamp light (with a steel or aluminum cone), a porcelain or coated glass infrared light, or an undertank heater will suffice. Some cold climates need both an undertank heater and an overhead heat source to reach proper temperatures (see individual species accounts). Start with a 25-watt incandescent bulb, increasing wattage if necessary to reach the proper temperature for the species you keep. Regular household incandescent bulbs work fine. Though bulbs made for reptiles are more expensive, they distribute heat better and thus may be more efficient. Use a timer to set the photoperiod. A red or blue 25-watt incandescent bulb is great for observing your gecko at night, as geckos will not be bothered by these lights. These colored bulbs do not produce as much heat as standard lamps, so they're perfectly suited to maintain the necessary nighttime temperature of about 65 degrees Fahrenheit (18 degrees Celsius).

Decorate with a few live succulents (short and without thorns) or with fake plants. Plants make an aesthetically pleasing vivarium display, and the geckos like to climb on them. Pieces of driftwood, cork bark, and rocks also work well. (Make sure stacked rocks are glued together with silicone cement so they don't topple over onto your delicate pets.) Do not give the geckos a "ramp" to the top of the vivarium, as this is the easiest way to escape; they will climb to the top and may muscle off the cage lid.

Your geckos need a couple items to hide in or under, where they cannot be seen. Put one hiding place near the cool end of the vivarium, the other near the warm end. Paper-towel rolls provide a nice low-budget option, as do short pieces of naturally curled cork bark. Your pet shop is likely to have many attractive hide boxes that will be used by eyelid geckos.

Feeding

Eyelid geckos are insectivorous and carnivorous, eating a variety of insects and other small prey (such as pinky mice). The diet should be varied, changing the food menu occasionally to prevent boredom and keep the feeding response sharp. Your gecko will perk up when a new food item is presented to it!

Adults of larger species, such as leopard and fat-tailed geckos, eat half-grown to adult crickets. Feed adults three or four times weekly, ten to twelve crickets per feeding. Feedings may be increased in frequency in warm weather or decreased in cooler weather. Larger *Coleonyx* species, such as *C. elegans,* will eat three-week-old crickets. Small species, such as *C. brevis* and *C. mitratus,* eat two-week-old (¼-in, 6-mm) crickets.

Full-grown mealworms will be taken by larger eyelid geckos. Juvenile mealworms can be fed to smaller geckos. Every day, put fresh worms into a dish shallow enough for the geckos to reach, and put a vitamin supplement in the dish with worms. Many breeders use mealworms as the staple diet, though others feel they contain too much indigestible chitin and phosphorus to make a satisfactory food.

Superworms can serve as treats for larger adult leopard and fat-tailed geckos, and waxworms make a great snack food for large species. Leopards are notorious for becoming addicted to waxworms (which are very high in fat), so be sure to limit their feeding. If wax worms are fed too often, your gecko will likely begin to refuse other food items, and then you will face the task of weaning the gecko off the high-fat wax worms and back to more nutritious food items.

Some adult leopard and fat-tailed geckos will take pinky mice as an occasional snack.

The usual calcium and vitamin supplementation should be given, especially to rapidly growing young. Giving calcium powder in a separate dish (see also chapter 3) is critical for females to avoid hypocalcemia and produce fertile eggs. Be sure to feed crickets and other live foods with a good brand of gut-loading food or nutritious leafy greens (or both) so they carry a wide array of vitamins and nutrients.

Breeding

On average, male eublepharids are sexually mature at seven months, females at nine months. *Eublepharis macularius* and *Hemitheconyx caudicinctus* should weigh a minimum of approximately 1.4 ounces (40 grams) before breeding. During the winter, dropping the temperature five to ten degrees Fahrenheit (dropping about three to six degrees Celsius) from warm season temperatures helps facilitate breeding in the spring. Female leopard geckos are "sperm retainers" and only need to be fertilized once or twice a season to produce fertile eggs the whole breeding season, which is during the warmer months of the year. Two soft-shelled, leathery eggs are produced about thirty days after mating and usually buried in the substrate. The eggs are visible through the abdomen as white oval bulges, slightly offset from each other, a few days before laying occurs. A female may lay four or more clutches of eggs per year.

For many eublepharids, a hide box that holds humidity well is a favored laying site. Fill a margarine tub with about 2 inches (5 cm) of moist vermiculite or sphagnum moss and cut a hole in the center of the lid just big enough for the gecko to enter. Check every few days to make sure the tub is still moist and clean and to look for eggs.

Egg Management

The eggs should be collected as soon as possible since they tend to desiccate if left in the open. Remove the eggs from the vivarium and place them in a clear plastic deli cup at least 3 inches (7.5 cm) tall with approximately 2 inches (5 cm) of moist vermiculite (1:1 mix with water by weight), perlite, or sphagnum moss in the bottom. Bury the eggs with a quarter of their tops showing and at least ½ inch (12.7 mm) apart. Most eublepharid species, as far as known, can be safely incubated at 80°F (27°C). Smaller species incubated at this temperature may hatch out as soon as forty-five to sixty days, larger species a bit later, but usually before one hundred days. Check the incubation medium frequently for a proper relative humidity of 70 to 80 percent. Moisten as needed, but do not overmoisten or hatchlings will drown in the egg due to excessive water absorption (the eggs turn reddish in that case). If eggs develop a dent, it is usually an indicator they are too dry. Spray water directly on dry eggs and repeat every few hours until the dent "pops" back out. Good eggs look good, bad eggs look bad. Keep questionable eggs at least a hundred days before throwing them out. Many novice gecko keepers throw out eggs too soon.

Incubating in a plastic container, these leopard gecko eggs are labeled to avoid confusion. The sex of hatchling leopard geckos and African fat-tailed geckos (*Hemitheconyx caudicinctus*) is determined by the temperature at which the eggs are incubated.

Hatchling Management

Hatchling eyelid geckos are very hardy, provided they are cared for properly. They will be quite defensive and noisy for approximately the first three months of their lives. This is normal behavior for youngsters, so do not be alarmed. They usually have a banded color pattern at first. As they age, their final colors and patterns develop, which may take a year or more. A hatchling can be kept in a small plastic or glass vivarium. Clutch mates can be kept together as long as they are about the same size—separate them if they fight. Use paper towels for the substrate and lengths of cardboard paper-towel rolls for hiding places.

A simple vivarium is easy to keep clean and makes it possible to monitor the hatchlings' food intake. Soda bottle caps work well as water and food dishes and can be disposed of when they are dirty. Feed small food items daily—for example, crickets and tiny mealworms. Supply calcium and vitamin supplementation as you would for adults, dusting in the typical fashion (see also chapter 4).

Give the babies access to a basking light or an under-tank heater, keeping the vivarium temperature between 81°F and 88°F (27°C and 31°C). It's easy to overheat small vivaria, so be careful. Mist one end of the vivarium daily to provide humidity until the babies are large enough for a small, moist hide box.

Hatchling leopard geckos, such as the one perched on a rock with an adult leopard, grow quickly and develop the adult color pattern in less than a year. Young leopards are hardy little lizards that feed well and don't need lots of heat.

Notes on Selected Species

Almost any pet shop has leopard geckos for sale, and many stores carry African fat-tails. It is harder to find the species of *Coleonyx* at pet shops, as these geckos are not as commonly bred in captivity.

Leopard Gecko
Eublepharis macularius

This is the best beginner gecko, requiring no previous experience.

Leopard geckos are found from western India to Afghanistan and Iraq, though the ancestors of the common species came mostly from Pakistan and western India. (Other species of leopard geckos exist but seldom are imported.) The natural habitat of the leopard gecko is in arid to semi-arid climates in regions, with sandy clay soil and rocky terrain where vegetation is sparse and consists of mostly tuft grasses and low shrubs.

This large species has a stocky body with a tail that stores fat. Normally patterned (wild-type) leopards have a creamy, yellowish white base color with irregular black spots creating two to three indistinct bands across the back. Leopard geckos are sexually dimorphic in that males are usually larger than females and have a heavier bone structure as well as more prominent femoral pores.

The normally patterned leopard gecko (top) is bright yellow with only a few blackish spots. The patternless morph (bottom) lacks black spots and much of the yellow pigment. A leucistic morph would lack all yellow color as well.

Leopard geckos produce incredibly colorful morphs, including this extreme high-yellow form. This is a xanthic mutation because the dark pigments are absent and the yellow is increased.

Since the 1990s, breeders have been producing stunning leopard gecko morphs, with eye color varying among these morphs. Normal eye color is brown, but morphs may have red or black eyes. (See de Vosjoli, Tremper, and Klingenberg 2005 for a thorough discussion of morphs and their evolution.) Some popular morphs are:

- Albino or amelanistic: These geckos lack the ability to produce dark pigments, which lets the brighter pigments shine through.
- Blizzard: This is a patternless mutation with white, brownish, yellowish, or pale blue-black colors.
- Ghost: In this morph, the dark primary colors fade with age.
- High-yellow: This morph is characterized by brilliant yellow colors and a reduced number and size of blackish spots; it may occur in combination with other morphs.
- Jungle: An irregular, aberrant pattern is present, unlike the wild-type's typical banding.
- Lavender: Distinct purple tints are present.
- Leucistic: Totally white and patternless, without any yellow or brown pigment.
- Melanistic: Opposite of amelanism, this morph is mostly black in color.
- Orange: This morph includes hypomelanistic (a reduced amount of dark pigment but not a complete lack thereof) and carrot-tail (tail at least 30 percent orange; Ray Hines, original breeder).

When a leopard gecko such as the one shown here develops more black pigment than normal and appears mostly blackish, it is called a melanistic morph.

- Snow or White: This morph retains black and white pattern from hatchling to adult.
- Giant (size morph): Adult females may weigh 3 ½ ounces (100 grams) or more, while adult males may weigh 5 ¼ ounces (150 grams) or more.

The leopard gecko is very hardy and easy to care for. These qualities, as well as its friendly nature, make *Eublepharis macularius* a great choice for beginners of all ages. Most eight-year-old children are ready to assume at least partial responsibility for a leopard gecko after they have been shown how to care for one.

You can keep one or two juveniles or one adult in a 10-gallon (38-L) glass vivarium or 16-quart (15.2-L) or bigger plastic storage container with quarter-inch (6-mm) holes for ventilation. One to three adults will do nicely in a 15-gallon (57-L) or larger vivarium or a 30-quart (28.5-L) or larger plastic storage container with appropriate air holes. When selecting more than one leopard gecko to keep in the same vivarium, make sure they are of similar size and there is only one adult male to a vivarium. Separate them if they fight or if one is losing weight. I have had success with male-female pairs, trios of two females and a male, and trios of females. Maintaining more than three adult leopards in one vivarium is difficult unless the cage is very large (at least 30 gallons, 114 L).

An undertank heater works well with glass vivaria and, with caution, may be used with some plastic storage containers. Temperatures should produce a thermal gradient, with the temperatures at the warmest end from 86°F to 88°F (30°C to 31°C) and at the cool end as low as 70°F to 75°F (21°C to 24°C) during the day. Nighttime lows should not exceed 65°F (18°C). Leopard geckos don't need a basking lamp, though they will use one on occasion. Similarly, a UV-B source is not necessary, but many keepers feel it doesn't hurt to provide one.

Every vivarium should have at least two hiding places—one on the warm side, one on the cool side. You can use hide boxes from the pet shop or give lengths of driftwood or cork bark. Leopard geckos like to climb on low objects such as driftwood and rocks.

Once females reach about 1.4 ounces (40 grams), they may be bred. The first clutch of eggs is laid approximately thirty days from breeding. Place the eggs in the moist incubation medium of choice (vermiculite, perlite, or sphagnum moss). Beginning gecko breeders should not attempt incubating eggs over 80°F (27°C) because egg management will be more difficult. (Eggs kept at higher temperatures tend to dry out more quickly than a beginner would notice.) It is interesting, though, to learn about advanced breeding practices. Leopard geckos exhibit temperature-dependent sex determination, with lower incubation temperatures producing mostly females and higher temperatures producing mostly males. Advanced breeders may incubate at specific temperatures to achieve the desired sex. Further, leopard geckos have been found to have pattern II sex determination, which means there are two approximate pivotal temperatures affecting the sex ratio of females and males produced (Viets et al. 1994). When eggs are incubated between 75°F and 86°F (24°C and 30°C), mostly females will hatch. The first pivotal temperature is 87°F (31°C), at which point the sex ratio of male to female will be approximately equal. As temperature increases from the first pivotal point to the second, 93°F (34°C), the number of males produced gradually increases until nearly all eggs hatch males. Above the second pivotal temperature, the ratio returns to favor females, though few eggs hatch at such high temperatures.

There is an inverse relationship between temperature and incubation length: Lower temperatures result in greater incubation times, from about seventy-five days at approximately 80°F (27°C). As temperatures increase, incubation time decreases to as few as thirty-six days at 90°F (32°C). Brightness of color also increases as the temperature rises. There are many variables affecting the babies long before they hatch, including the mother and the temperature of the nest site she chooses (W. Bragg et al. 2000). Usually clutch mates hatch within three days of each other.

Once hatchlings appear, you can place one or two hatchlings in an opaque shoebox-size plastic container with air holes drilled in the sides for air circulation. Another option is a 5- to 10-gallon (19- to 38-L) vivarium. Provide heat in the same ways as for adults, but be extremely careful not to overheat small hatchlings—their small bodies are not as tolerant of hot temperatures and thus are more vulnerable to overheating. Keep the babies on a paper-towel substrate with paper-towel rolls for hiding places. Clean the enclosure frequently, and make sure fresh water is available at all times in a clean container.

Feed two-week-old crickets or small mealworms (placed in a very shallow dish) daily, about five to ten insects for each hatchling. Add supplements to food each feeding, and remove uneaten food after about twenty minutes. Spray one end of the vivarium daily with water to create humidity. Once the babies are eating three-week-old crickets, you can give them a humid hide box. Separate them if there is weight loss or fighting and tail loss.

Texas Banded Gecko
Coleonyx brevis

This species is suggested for novice keepers with some reptile experience, as it is a bit more delicate than the species recommended for beginners.

The Texas banded has a limited range in the United States—in southwestern Texas, southeastern New Mexico, and northeastern Mexico. It lives in deserts and arid regions with intense sunlight, though it is active only at night.

This is a small, slender eublepharid with reddish brown bands on a creamy yellowish background with some spotting.

Though slender and small (seldom reaching 5 inches, 12.7 cm), the Texas banded gecko is a very hardy species and is usually calm when handled. Management is essentially the same as for the leopard gecko, allowing for size. Smaller vivaria may be used; one or two adult specimens can live happily in a 5-gallon (19-L) vivarium. The substrate should be a fine grade of sand. Adults feed on small crickets, very small mealworms, and similar foods.

The eggs should be incubated at 80°F (27°C). *Coleonyx* species exhibit genotypic sex-determination (the sex being determined at fertilization), so there is no advantage to incubating at higher or lower temperatures and risking unsuccessful incubation. Hatchlings are managed in much the same way as leopard geckos, except their food is much smaller—pinhead crickets instead of the two-week size for their larger cousins.

Yucatan Banded Gecko
Coleonyx elegans

This species is for the advanced keeper with considerable reptile experience.

As would be expected from the common name, this species is found in eastern Mexico (the Yucatan Peninsula), but it also ranges widely over southwestern Mexico and then south over Central America as far as El Salvador. In most of this range, it prefers relatively moist habitats, including tropical forest floors as well as caves and ruins.

Unlike more common banded geckos, the Yucatan banded gecko (*Coleonyx elegans*) is found in humid tropical environments. This must be reflected in the way its vivarium is set up.

This is a slender gecko with a creamy white background color and reddish brown bands and spots like most other species of the genus. The patterns of some specimens can be quite aberrant, displaying stripes and spots. The young have a bright orange background color, which gradually fades to white at adulthood. It grows to about 6 inches (15 cm).

Yucatan banded geckos are exotic, nervous eyelid geckos that do not like to be handled. They need the standard leopard gecko vivarium and decorations, yet adjusted for size and habitat. A 10-gallon (38-L) glass or plastic vivarium will do for a pair or trio of adults. Do not put more than one male in a vivarium as males do not tolerate each other. The substrate should be 70 percent sphagnum moss and 30 percent fine sand to provide the relative humidity (70 to 80 percent) this species needs. Cypress mulch has also been successfully used because it holds humidity and allows tunneling. I also have used 2 inches (5 cm) of sphagnum moss topped by a medium grade orchid bark. Temperatures should be 75°F to 84°F (24°C to 29°C) during the day and never below 65°F (18°C) at night. Spray the sides of the vivarium with water daily.

This species especially favors waxworms (remember, feed only as a snack), which are good to get them into breeding condition over the winter. Three-week-old crickets work well as a standard diet. Hatchlings are extremely delicate and need misting at least twice or more daily to keep their humidity at the proper level. Feed them week-old crickets. As soon as they are eating two-week-old crickets, set up a small moist hide box for them.

Central American Banded Gecko
Coleonyx mitratus
This is an intermediate species for the keeper with some gecko experience.

Coleonyx mitratus, the Central American banded gecko, is a bit less nervous than the Yucatan banded gecko and thus harder to stress. However, banded geckos in general seldom appreciate being handled.

Coleonyx mitratus is a species of tropical Central America, ranging from Guatemala and Honduras to Panama and found in moist habitats, usually on or near the forest floor.

This eyelid gecko is smaller and more slender than *C. elegans,* with creamy white background coloration and black bands, spots, and aberrant patterns.

Like *C. elegans, C. mitratus* is a nervous species that does not like to be handled; however, it has a slightly calmer disposition and therefore is easier to keep. Care for it much as you would *C. elegans,* bearing in mind that its smaller size requires smaller food—pinhead crickets for hatchlings, and two-week-old crickets for adults.

Western Banded Gecko
Coleonyx variegatus

This is a gecko for the novice with some reptile experience.

One of the smaller geckos commonly kept, the western banded gecko (*Coleonyx variegatus*) is rather easy to keep in a dry vivarium. If possible, try to find captive-bred specimens.

Coleonyx variegatus is found widely across the southwestern United States from Southern California to New Mexico and also in northwestern Mexico. It prefers deserts and arid regions with intense sunlight, yet it is nocturnal, commonly seen near homes and crossing highways at night.

This species is similar to *C. brevis* but with different details of the femoral pores and scale counts. Its coloration is quite variable, with some populations showing more distinct banding or spotting than others.

The Western banded can be kept and bred much as the Texas banded. This species is commonly collected in the spring and early summer and sold at low prices in the United States. Captive-bred specimens also are available.

African Fat-Tailed Gecko
Hemitheconyx caudicinctus

This is a great gecko for the novice who has some reptile experience.

African fat-tailed geckos are found over much of West Africa, from Senegal and Mali to Nigeria and Cameroon. They are a species of semi-arid savannahs and bushlands and spend the day in moist burrows.

This African fat-tailed gecko specimen (*Hemitheconyx caudicinctus*) shows an obviously regenerated tail. African fat-tailed geckos are much like heavy-set leopard geckos in appearance and personality.

As you might expect from the name, this is a thick-bodied eyelid gecko with a thick tail that stores fat; in captivity and as a wild-caught gecko, it often has a partially regenerated tail (likely due to fighting with other African fat-tails). The common pattern is of two wide, dark, reddish brown bands on the back against a pale reddish brown to yellowish background. Some specimens have a narrow white stripe down the center of the back. Amelanistic morphs (lacking dark coloration) exist.

The African fat-tail is relatively easy to care for and widely available. It tends to stress more easily than the leopard gecko when handled, but it is an excellent pet. Apply the same instruction for cages, pairings, temperatures, and feeding schedules as for the leopards. The substrate, however, should be sphagnum moss topped with a medium grade orchid bark for increased moisture. Breeding and hatchling management are the same as for the leopard gecko. In fact, many novice breeders like to keep the two species together, but this is not recommended as the two do not live in the same environments in the wild, fat-tails needing a bit more moisture than leopard geckos do.

CHAPTER 7
DAY GECKOS

Day geckos belong to the genus *Phelsuma*, which consists of more than sixty described species and subspecies. Most *Phelsuma* occur on Madagascar, a beautiful and environmentally diverse island located in the Indian Ocean east of Africa. Many species also are found on the surrounding islands of the Comoros, Mauritius, Reunion, and the Seychelles. A few species live some distance away from Madagascar, as far north as the Andaman Islands in the Bay of Bengal (*Phelsuma andamanensis*) and on the eastern coast of Africa in and near Tanzania (*P. dubia* and *P. parkeri*). All *Phelsuma* species are protected by the Convention on International Trade in Endangered Species of Wild Fauna and Flora (CITES), which strives to protect plants and animals from commercial exploitation and, to some extent, environmental losses that are a reality in Madagascar, where forests are rapidly lost to development.

Some of the most colorful and popular day geckos, such as the blue-tailed day gecko (*Phelsuma cepediana*) seen here, are expensive and most suitable for advanced keepers. Only a few are appropriate for beginning keepers.

The giant day gecko (*Phelsuma madagascariensis grandis*) and Standing's day gecko (*P. standingi*) are the largest lizards in the genus, the biggest individuals ranging from 9 to 11 inches (23 to 28 cm) long. Medium-size species, such as the gold dust day gecko (*P. laticauda*), are about 5 to 9 inches (12.7 to 23 cm) long. The neon day gecko (*P. klemmeri*) is considered a small species at about 4 inches (10 cm) long. Large species are known to live as long as thirty years, whereas smaller species live ten to twelve years on average.

Standing's day gecko *(Phelsuma standingi)* is unusual among species of the genus because it comes from relatively dry forests in Madagascar, making it an easier species to keep.

Day geckos are diurnal (active during the day), with many species recognized by their bright, sometimes fluorescent, colors. They are fast-moving compared with most geckos and have no problem scampering up vertical glass surfaces with their sticky feet with wide pads. They make great display geckos in a well-planted, tropical vivarium with an adequate basking spot. *Phelsuma* species prefer not to be handled and should not be grabbed due to their delicate skin.

Housing

Day geckos do best in a vertically oriented tropical vivarium, as described in Chapter 3. The basic requirements are a tall glass vivarium (which helps retain humidity), plants, and good lighting.

Glass vivaria with a side-opening screen door, in addition to a top-screened opening, are preferred, as *Phelsuma* species like to bask at the top of the vivarium near the basking light. This makes vivaria that only open from the top exceedingly vulnerable to escapes. Keep small, soft bird or fish nets handy to catch escapees. Vivaria should be a minimum of 10 gallons (38 L) for small to medium species and 20 gallons (76 L) or more for large species. Vivaria made completely from screening may be used outdoors in environments that maintain at least 50 percent relative humidity, but you must carefully monitor the temperature. Outdoor vivaria must be made of screen (glass enclosures hold in heat and thus can "cook" the gecko) and kept in the shade (direct sunlight will kill your gecko!). Be careful of predators such as ants and cats.

Decorations are essential because most species like to sit on or hide in live plants. Use *Sansevieria* (mother-in-law's tongue), philodendron, or pothos. For additional hiding spots, include lengths of bamboo or PVC pipe slightly larger in diameter than the geckos are at mid-body. At least one piece should be place diagonally, with another placed horizontally, if possible. For substrate, use 2 to 3 inches (5 to 7.5 cm) of mulch topped by a thick layer of orchid bark of an appropriate grade for your specific geckos: medium to large grade for larger individuals, fine grade for smaller individuals.

You will need a large, vertical vivarium, such as this 45-gallon hexagonal tank, that can house living plants as well as the lizards if you plan on keeping a pair of Madagascan giant day geckos (*Phelsuma madagascariensis grandis*).

A basking lamp is essential, too. Most *Phelsuma* species need a basking spot that reaches between 86°F and 88°F (30°C and 31°C). Use a metal clip-on lamp to hold a household incandescent bulb of appropriate wattage. Choose one with a width of at least 8½ inches (22 cm) or so in diameter, so it will not tip over easily from its position above the vivarium. Supply a fluorescent lamp bright enough to keep the vivarium well lit during the day as bright light is critical to *Phelsuma* health. A reptile full-spectrum bulb supplying both UV-A and UV-B is fine, but large amounts of UV-B do not seem to be necessary for healthy day geckos that receive a well-supplemented diet. Combination bulbs (full-spectrum plus incandescent) are available, but these types may be too hot. Use a timer to turn lights on at sunrise and off at sundown.

If the vivarium temperature drops below 65°F (18°C), add nighttime lighting to supply heat when the incandescent lamp is off. Sometimes the addition of a red or blue incandescent bulb is enough to bring the temperature up. Alternative methods include infrared lighting, such as the porcelain or coated-glass night-lights or heat emitters widely sold in pet shops. Another option is to fill a glass jar with water, then place a submersible fish-tank heater (set to your gecko's favorite temperature) inside the jar and a stick-on tape thermometer on the outside of the jar. Place aluminum foil over the top of the jar to ensure the gecko cannot enter the water and drown.

To add humidity to the vivarium, mist with water from a spray bottle or use a more elaborate misting system such as those sold for keeping chameleons (check with your pet shop). Day geckos need to be misted once or twice daily, depending on the humidity requirements of the species. *Phelsuma* species prefer to drink droplets of water from plant leaves and the sides of the vivarium.

Feeding

Day geckos are insectivorous (insect eating) and frugivorous (fruit eating). The diet for a *Phelsuma* species should consist of a variety of items.

Crickets are the main dietary staple of day geckos. Remember to match the size of the food to the size of the gecko. Large species eat three- to five-week-old ($^3/_8$-inch to $^5/_8$-inch, 10-mm to 16-mm) crickets. Small to medium species eat two-week-old ($^1/_2$-inch, 12.7-mm) crickets. Feed adults three or four times weekly, ten to twelve crickets per gecko each feeding. Feedings may be increased in frequency during the warm season or decreased in cooler weather when the geckos are not as active. Adjust the feeding schedule to suit the gecko.

Other usable insect foods are mealworms, superworms, and waxworms—the larva make great snacks for larger gecko species. Small moths, commercially available fruit flies, and small cockroaches are great "entertainment" food that small day geckos will chase.

Fruit purees from commercial mixes or real fruits (especially fruits that grow in Madagascar, such as banana, papaya, and mango) will be taken from small cups placed in the upper parts of the vivarium. Soda bottle caps and walnut shells work well for this purpose. Feed purees once a week in place of an insect feeding.

Day geckos need dietary supplementation for calcium and vitamins. A reliable combination is two parts Rep-Cal calcium with vitamin D_3 to one part Herptivite multivitamins. Additional calcium powder in a small dish is critical for females to avoid hypocalcemia and produce fertile eggs. However, day geckos kept outdoors need not be given supplements with vitamin D_3, as the sun provides this naturally.

Breeding

Mating and egg-laying occur mostly during the warmer parts of the year, though *Phelsuma* species may lay eggs year round, slowing down reproductively during winter. You should use a sexually mature breeding pair or trio (one male and two females). Females may start breeding when around nine months old, males at about seven months. Day geckos are thought to be "sperm retainers" that need to be fertilized just once each breeding season to produce a whole season of eggs. Two white, hard-shelled

This hatching Madagascan giant day gecko should not be put back into the vivarium with its parents—it could be mistaken for food.

eggs are laid about thirty days after mating, with more clutches following every few weeks. During the peak of breeding season, day geckos can lay a clutch as often as every fourteen days.

Some species "glue" their eggs to the substrate. Most day geckos are not gluers. However, the blue-tailed day gecko (*Phelsuma cepediana*), which is a gluer, typically sticks her eggs to the vivarium glass or to another firm, vertical area. This makes catching the babies when they hatch more difficult for you than with nongluer eggs that are simply laid on the substrate or in the base of a plant, where they can be collected and hatched in a separate container.

Egg Management
Whenever possible, *Phelsuma* eggs should be collected and incubated separately from the parents because the parents might eat the hatchlings. Certainly do not remove the eggs if the eggs are glued, as they will usually break if you try to pry them off the surface they are stuck to. Glued eggs should be isolated by putting some sterile medical gauze over them with tape around the edges. If they are laid in a bamboo tube, then tape gauze on the ends of the tube and put the tube in an incubator, or leave it in with the parents. This method allows the eggs to breathe and benefit from the humidity and also allows you to monitor their status through the gauze. Once the babies hatch, collect them and

set them up in a separate vivarium. Eggs that aren't glued are more easily collected. Once you locate the eggs, put them in a bottle cap in a separate container, such as a clear plastic 16-ounce (0.47-L) deli cup with a lid and air holes. This will serve as the incubator.

The eggs should be incubated at about 70 percent relative humidity. Use a hygrometer (available at electronics stores and reptile specialty shops) to measure humidity; don't guess. There are many different ways to achieve this level of humidity. You can use approximately 2 inches (5 cm) of moist vermiculite, perlite, or sphagnum moss placed in the bottom of the container, with the eggs in their bottle cap sitting on top. Check the substrate periodically to make sure it is moist enough. Err on the dry side because babies will drown in the egg if it is too moist.

Most *Phelsuma* species may be safely incubated in the 80°F to 88°F (27°C to 31°C) temperature range. Day geckos exhibit temperature-dependent sex determination, in which lower relative temperatures produce females, higher temperatures produce males, and middle temperatures produce a mix of both sexes. Find a place in your home (such as a shelf in a warm corner, the gecko's vivarium, or an incubator) to put the eggs for their incubation period. The important part is the correct temperature range—not a fancy incubator.

Look for the babies to hatch as early as forty-five days (smaller species) or as long as seventy days (larger species).

As incubation temperature increases, time to hatching decreases, but temperatures that are too warm may end up killing the embryos.

Hatchling Management

Hatchling *Phelsuma* require more frequent misting and smaller food items offered more frequently than do adults. Because the hatchlings are so small, they are at risk of dehydration, but this is easy to avoid with the proper vivarium setup.

For small- to medium-size *Phelsuma* species (such as *P. cepediana* and *P. klemmeri*), transfer hatchlings by encouraging them to hop onto a strip of paper towel and then carefully moving them while on the paper towel. Do not handle them because they are too small and delicate at this size; picking hatchlings up with your fingers could easily crush them. For housing, use a 16-ounce (0.47-L) clear deli cup with small air holes. Place a few strips of paper towel inside to create a place for the gecko to sit and hide. Mist the sides of the container (not the paper towel) once daily so the young gecko will get a drink and proper humidity at the same time. Change the towels and container frequently in order to keep things clean. Keep the container under bright fluorescent lighting and at the

Hatchling geckos, such as this young Madagascan giant day gecko, eat their first shed skin (and sometimes part of the egg shell).

Keep juvenile day geckos singly in small plastic vivaria with paper on the bottom to make sure they are feeding well and to prevent fighting between the siblings.

lower end of the adult basking temperature range (about 85°F, 29.5°C), with nighttime temperatures between 70°F and 75°F (21°C and 24°C).

Feed smaller hatchlings daily with five or six pinhead crickets to start. Fruit puree or commercial day gecko food can be given two or three times weekly, using a bottle cap as a dish. When the hatchlings graduate to week-old crickets, you can move them into a small glass vivarium with a screen top (use the same setup as for adults, just smaller). The screen must be fine enough so they can't escape. Clutch mates can be kept together in this setup as long as they don't fight and they are similar in size.

For larger species, the hatchlings should be transferred to a new container using paper towels as described above or a small fish net. As the hatchlings grow, move them to a small glass vivarium or plastic critter box or similar premade enclosure. Keep the hatchlings either in clutch pairs or individually. Remove clutch mates that become aggressive or that grow significantly larger than the other specimens. Use the same temperature ranges as for small and medium day geckos.

Feed larger hatchlings one-week-old crickets to start; hatchlings will graduate to two-week-old crickets in just a week. Feed the same fruit and day gecko food mix regimen described above. Mist the sides of the container and plants twice daily.

Notes on Selected Species

Day geckos featured in this book were chosen for their easy care and wide availability to potential gecko keepers, with one exception—*Phelsuma cepediana*, the spectacular blue-tailed day gecko, our first subject below. This gecko is very delicate and quite rare in captivity, but it is included because many novices are attracted to its amazing beauty.

Blue-Tailed Day Gecko
Phelsuma cepediana

This species is for advanced *Phelsuma* keepers only.

One of the most beautiful, but most difficult to keep, day geckos is the blue-tailed day gecko (*Phelsuma cepediana*).

This beautiful species is widely distributed on Mauritius, one of the Mascarene Islands east of Madagascar, but it also has been introduced into the neighboring island of Rodrigues and even to the Ivolonia area of Madagascar. It is found in both coastal areas and the interior—at low, middle, and high elevations—and it adapts well to areas disturbed by humans as long as sufficient vegetation is left. Unfortunately, within the past four hundred years, most of the natural vegetation on Mauritius has been destroyed and replaced with sugar cane and other agricultural crops, and these day geckos cannot live in areas totally converted to agricultural use. *P. cepediana* can be found on trees and bushes, including coconut palms, bananas, papayas, and traveler's palms. Healthy populations occur on banana trees and other backyard vegetation in suburban areas of some villages and towns. Blue-tails prefer less arid areas and are found in very high densities in suitable habitats where there is high rainfall or sufficient moisture.

The blue-tailed day is a medium-size species. Males average 4 ½ to 5 ½ inches (11.4 to 14 cm), with large specimens reaching 6 inches (15.2 cm); females average 3 ¾ to 4 ½ inches (9.5 to 11.4 cm). Females are extremely delicate.

One of the most brilliantly colored day geckos, *P. cepediana* is a sexually dimorphic species. When at peak coloration, males are typically brilliant blue above, with large, irregularly placed red spots and dashes. A red dorsolateral stripe, which may or may not be broken, is always present on the side, and a red eye stripe extends from the back of the nostril to the shoulder. The flanks are a bright chartreuse, the tail deep blue. Females are bright green with rust-colored spotting. A rust-colored dorsolateral stripe and typical eye stripe are always present. Females from the upland populations frequently have brighter reds and reduced striping and may have a cluster of small red spots on the lower back.

This species is best kept in vertically oriented enclosures with live plants such as potted banana trees, *Dracaena*, bromeliads, philodendron, or birds of paradise. It is essential to use a well-planted enclosure with this species and to keep humidity levels up while affording sufficient air flow. Accomplish this by watering and heavily misting major portions of the enclosure twice daily. House the geckos as pairs. The blue-tailed and other delicate day gecko species do much better if housed in screened outdoor enclosures with large potted plants during late spring, summer, and early fall, when the temperatures are in the 70°F to 90°F (21°C to 32°C) range. If your winter outdoor temperatures are in this range, you may continue to keep your gecko outside. If the temperature dips below the acceptable range, bring your gecko inside. Be sure there are areas that afford both sun and shade in these enclosures.

This species is an egg-gluer. Females lay best with generous and frequent offerings of fruit purees (Christenson and Christenson 2003) and commercial mixes; you will need to add fruit to most commercial mixes, as they are not sweet enough for this gecko.

Yellow-Headed Day Gecko
Phelsuma klemmeri

For the intermediate keeper with some *Phelsuma* experience.

Yellow-headed day geckos (*Phelsuma klemmeri*) are among the smallest day gecko species. They also are very quick and hardy for their size.

Coastal northwestern Madagascar is home to this species, which lives on large trees in rain forests and, if alarmed, will retreat into crevices in the bark.

The head and neck are iridescent yellow with small black speckles. The upper and middle back are bright turquoise blue, and the lower back and uppermost portion of the tail are light brown with the rest of the tail turquoise blue. A large black spot is present behind the eye, followed by a broad, black dorsolateral stripe that extends the length of the body. The body is laterally flattened, considerably more so than in other day geckos. One of the smallest species of day geckos, the yellow-head is about $3\frac{1}{4}$ to $3\frac{3}{4}$ inches (8.3 to 9.5 cm) long.

Keep this species in a well-planted vivarium with a number of closely packed bamboo sections placed in the vegetation for perching sites. Bromeliads and orchids are well suited to this species. These geckos can be kept in sexual pairs or trios. Daytime temperatures should range between 85°F and 95°F (29.5°C and 35°C), with a nighttime low of 68°F (20°C). Mist both morning and evening. The diet should mainly consist of two-week-old crickets. You may also feed these day geckos vestigial-winged fruit flies, wax moths, and small wax moth larvae (waxworms).

Generally, yellow-headed day geckos are a hardy species despite their small size.

This species is not an egg-gluer. Eggs are somewhat oval in shape and hatch in thirty-nine to fifty-two days when incubated at 81°F (27°C), plus or minus four degrees Fahrenheit (two degrees Celsius). Hatchlings are extremely small, averaging only about one inch (23 to 28 mm). Hatchlings are paler in color than adults.

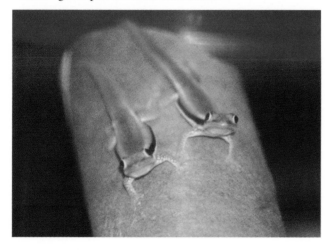

Another name for the yellow-headed day gecko is neon day gecko. In the proper light, healthy yellow-headed geckos can literally glow with color.

Gold Dust Day Gecko
Phelsuma laticauda laticauda

This is an intermediate species for keepers who have some reptile experience.

Found naturally on Madagascar and also the Comoro Islands, it has been introduced onto Farquhar Island in the southern Seychelles and to the Hawaiian Islands, where it is established on both sides of Oahu, the Kona side of the Big Island, and on Maui. It uses a variety of tropical plants, including pandanus, coconut palms, and birds of paradise, as well as human dwellings.

These medium-size day geckos have a background color of bright green to yellowish green, with light blue around the eyes. There are three red ovals on the back and brilliant yellow speckles (the gold dust) on the neck. The tail is slightly flattened. Adults are 4 to 5 inches (10 to 13 cm) long.

The gold dust day gecko (*Phelsuma laticauda laticauda*) is a popular species often bred in captivity. There can be considerable variation in the brightness of the color pattern.

These geckos prefer daytime temperatures of 82°F to 90°F (28°C to 32°C), with a ten- to twelve-degree Fahrenheit (six- to seven-degree Celsius) drop at night. In addition to full-spectrum lighting (with UV-B), include a 50- or 75-watt spot lamp for basking. The vivarium should have live plants plus vertical bamboo sections for egg-laying. As for all day geckos, good air flow is important. Provide water through misting the plants and vivarium glass sides on a daily basis.

Adults feed on two-week-old crickets, waxworms, and fruit flies, with a fruit supplement. Feed three times a week during most of the year and twice a week during a standard two-month winter cooling period when the temperature is allowed to drop to 70°F to 77°F (21°C to 25°C). Dust the insect food with a vitamin-mineral powder with calcium. As is common with other species of day geckos, females store excess calcium for their eggs in sacs at the sides of the neck. The females are ready to mate again right after laying the first clutch, so male-female sexual pairs should not be separated. As in some other day geckos, immediately after laying, the eggs are held with the hind feet until their shells harden (usually in a few hours). Like most other Madagascan day geckos, gold dust days are not egg-gluers. Usually two eggs (occasionally one), often stuck together, are laid in a protected location, such as at a plant leaf joint or inside a section of bamboo. Interestingly, with this species, if the eggs are not laid in a protected location, they are almost always infertile; in such circumstances, the eggs may be eaten by the female. Eggs may be incubated at 82°F (28°C) with high humidity and will take forty to forty-five days to hatch at this temperature.

The neonates are about 1½ inches (4 cm) long. They can be raised singly or in clutch mate pairs, in a small, planted vivarium. If a good nutritional balance is maintained, the lizards will be ready to breed within nine to twelve months. This species breeds well in captivity.

Angulated Gold Dust Day Gecko
Phelsuma laticauda angularis
This subspecies is for the intermediate keeper who has reptile experience.

This gecko is found only in northwestern Madagascar in the region around Antsohihy. There it occurs in palms, pandanus, and other pantropic vegetation.

It is smaller than the nominate form (averages 4 to 4½ inches, 10.2 to 11.4 cm, long), with a flatter, wider tail and less gold speckling. The number of femoral pores is reduced in males of this subspecies, and in place of the three large, red oval markings found on the back of *P. laticauda laticauda*, there is a wide, irregular, inverted V-shaped marking. Care instructions are the same as for *P. l. laticauda*.

Lined Day Gecko
Phelsuma lineata lineata
This is an intermediate gecko for keepers who have reptile experience.

Lined day geckos (*Phelsuma lineata lineata*) are modestly colored lizards; males such as this one carry most of the color in the form of fine red dots over the green back. The black line on the lower side, however, is not a common pattern in the genus.

This day gecko is found only on Madagascar on the central plateau—common around the capital city of Antananarivo—and lives in a variety of pantropic vegetation, including subtropical bushes and trees and on human dwellings.

It is a medium-size day gecko, with males typically an intense dark green with many tiny red dots over most of the back. The green background color of the female is more subdued. A black lateral stripe separates the green back from the whitish underside. Adults average about $4^3/_4$ inches (12 cm) long. Care instructions are the same as for *P. laticauda*.

Madagascan Giant Day Gecko
Phelsuma madagascariensis grandis

This species is an excellent choice for novice keepers with reptile experience.

Widely distributed in northern Madagascar, including several of the offshore islets, the Madagascan giant lives in a variety of palms and other tropical vegetation and is found around human dwellings.

Males average up to 11 inches (28 cm) long, with some recorded at 12 inches (30 cm), and have well-developed femoral pores under the hind legs. Females are a bit smaller. This species is typically bright green with a red eye stripe that extends from the nostril to the eye. Large red spots may be present on the back, but the degree of spotting depends entirely on the individual, rather than the geographic area from which it originates. A few of the most colorful specimens may have a little blue spotting along with wide red spots or bars. The vivarium for this large gecko should be planted with sturdy species such as snake plants (*Sansevieria*), which these lizards will readily use as resting, basking, and egg-laying sites. Horizontal bamboo strips and sections are useful for basking, too, and vertical bamboo stalks at least 2 inches (5 cm) in diameter and open at the top are useful for the female to retreat into and lay her eggs. These are excellent display animals that should be housed singly or in sexual pairs.

Although it may be a foot long and quite hardy, the Madagascan giant day gecko (*Phelsuma madagascariensis grandis*) must be handled with care to avoid injuries to its thin skin, which may slough off in patches if gripped too hard.

If you want to breed them, house a male and a female together throughout the year. Ideally, the female should be only slightly smaller than or equal to the size of the male, as courtship can be aggressive. The male will grab the skin along the female's neck in his mouth while copulating. Generally, a female should not be used for breeding unless she is at least one year old. If a female does not show proper courtship behavior, she may be attacked by the male, so compatibility of specimens is essential. If the pair is compatible, they should not be separated, as separation may lead to future aggression if they are placed together again. A female in an egg-laying cycle typically lays one or two eggs every four to six weeks. The heaviest breeding and egg-laying occur in the warm season. When the female is ready to lay, she will enter a section of bamboo, often lie on her back, and lay her eggs. She gently holds each egg with her rear feet until the shell has hardened (in a few hours). Eggs should be maintained at a temperature of 82°F (28°C) and at 75 percent relative humidity. With this regimen, the eggs will hatch in forty-seven to sixty-five days. The neonates are large, typically from 2½ to 2¾ inches (6.7 to 7 cm) long. It is best to raise each of the young separately in small vivaria.

Peacock or Four-Spot Day Gecko
Phelsuma quadriocellata quadriocellata
This is an intermediate species for keepers with *Phelsuma* experience.

Peacock day geckos (*Phelsuma quadriocellata*) have a pair of large black spots on each side of the body. Well-marked specimens also are covered with small red spots and have a blue tail.

This interesting species is found in eastern Madagascar, including the region around Perinet. It inhabits a variety of pantropic vegetation, including banana plants, and is found near human dwellings.

Typical adults of this medium-size species are forest green on the back with red dots and stripes. A blue, V-shaped marking may be present on the snout, and tiny blue speckles may be present on the neck. A large black or navy blue spot outlined in turquoise is present in the armpit area behind the front leg, with another dark area in front of the rear leg. Peacock day geckos average about 4 ³/₄ inches (12 cm) in length.

House them in a well-planted vertical vivarium. In addition to normal plantings, include vertical bamboo stalks with a diameter of ³/₄ inch (2 cm) that have the top segments partially open so the female can enter to lay eggs. Maintain these geckos at 82°F to 86°F (28°C to 30°C), with a nighttime drop in temperature to 68°F (20°C). This species likes high humidity—a 75-percent daytime humidity level is ideal, with a heavy misting in the evening. It breeds best during the months of July and August, when temperatures are allowed to drop to 75°F (24°C) during the day and to 60°F to 65°F (16°C to 18°C) at night. Only a single pair should be housed together.

If the female is in an egg-laying cycle, she will typically lay two eggs every three to five weeks, averaging about six sets of eggs a year. Usually, the eggs are deposited in the hollow vertical bamboo sections, but on occasion they will be attached to leaves. The eggs should be incubated at a temperature of 82°F (28°C) with about 75 percent relative humidity. Following this regimen, the eggs will take forty to forty-five days to hatch. The neonates average 1 ¼ inches (3 cm) in length and will take pinhead crickets, wingless fruit flies, and a fruit supplement.

Standing's Day Gecko
Phelsuma standingi

This is a good gecko for a novice with reptile experience.

Found in southwestern Madagascar, including the region around Andranolaho, this species inhabits the dry region of Madagascar, which has unique thorny forest vegetation. Until recently, this was one of the very few areas in Madagascar that was relatively undisturbed, but charcoal burners are making inroads into the habitat and destroying the vegetation. For this reason *P. standingi* is now a species of special concern to the world's conservation organizations.

Though hatchling day geckos generally look like their parents, baby Standing's day geckos (*Phelsuma standingi*) have a unique pattern of many reddish brown bands over the body and tail, which will break into the finely spotted pattern as they mature.

91

Hatchlings have a yellowish green head with a series of lines and bars. The neck and back are brown with a large number of thin, light-colored bands and bars extending over the back. These bands and bars become wider and more mint green on the tail. Adults of this species look quite different. Typically, adults are light gray with some pale turquoise on the head and tail and fine, gray reticulated markings on the head and body. An exceptionally marked adult is light turquoise with small gray reticulations on the head and back and light gray flanks and upper legs. Males can be distinguished from females by their large, well-developed, brown femoral pores. This is a very large, heavy-bodied day gecko that averages 8 1/4 to 10 inches (21 to 25 cm) long in both sexes, with exceptional specimens exceeding 11 inches (28 cm).

The enclosure for Standing's day gecko should be reasonably large with a vertical format. Be sure to add several sturdy, live potted plants, such as *Sansevieria*. This species does well and breeds readily in captivity. No more than one pair should be housed together.

Eggs are typically laid in plant leaf joints or under surface litter on the ground. When incubated at 82°F to 84°F (28°C to 29°C), eggs hatch in approximately seventy days. One of the keys to breeding this species is to provide a temperature drop at night. Daytime temperatures should be in the mid-eighties Farenheit (high twenties Celcius) with a small spotlight producing a basking spot in the mid-nineties Farenheit (about 35°C). Nighttime temperatures should drop to 72°F to 75°F (22°C to 24°C). This species may become quite accustomed to humans and, once it is well acclimated, often will accept calcium-dusted crickets and other insects from a person's fingers.

CHAPTER 8

MORE GECKOS OF MADAGASCAR

Madagascar is home to a diverse group of geckos and is one of the most beautiful and the most environmentally endangered reptile and amphibian habitats in existence. Madagascan day geckos (genus *Phelsuma*), leaf-tailed geckos (genus *Uroplatus*), and ground geckos (genus *Paroedura*) are commonly kept by gecko enthusiasts. We discussed *Phelsuma* species earlier, and now we will discuss the genera *Uroplatus* and *Paroedura*. Since *Uroplatus* species are arboreal and the *Paroedura* species of interest to keepers are terrestrial (many of the other species are arboreal, however), we will discuss them separately, beginning with *Uroplatus*.

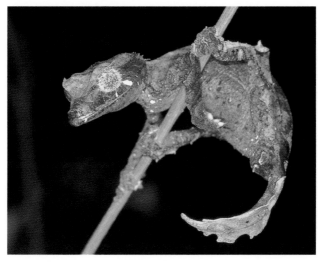

This leaf-mimicking satanic leaf-tailed gecko (*Uroplatus phantasticus*) is one of the stranger species found on the island of Madagascar, which is famous for its many unusual reptiles and amphibians.

Leaf-Tailed Geckos (Genus *Uroplatus*)

Uroplatus is a Madagascan endemic genus, all the ten or more species originating from Madagascar and adjacent offshore islands. They are outrageous looking lizards, and their behaviors are equally exciting. *Uroplatus* species are largely nocturnal and often are vocal during their active period at night. Their vocalizations range from soft calls in the smaller species to loud, piercing calls in the larger ones. These vocalizations are thought to be related to courtship and territorial and defensive behaviors. *Uroplatus* species exhibit another interesting behavior, tail-waving. This is thought to be related to vocalization behaviors and possibly to distract prey long enough to eat them. These geckos use their body shapes, colors, and patterns as camouflage to blend into their environment. When looking at *Uroplatus* geckos in the wild, it is hard to distinguish them from tree bark or branches. They sit very still during the day, and many sleep on a vertical surface such as a tree trunk with head pointing toward the ground as if ready to spring into action to grab an unsuspecting food item that may pass by. All *Uroplatus* species are arboreal, have adhesive lamellae (pads) under the toes, and have no problem climbing up trees and vertical glass surfaces. Their tails often are extremely flattened and oddly shaped and regenerate if broken off.

Though in many cultures geckos are considered good luck, *Uroplatus* species unfortunately do not share that privilege and are demonized by native peoples in Madagascar; this is no doubt due to the animals' bizarre physical appearances, activity at night, and strange calling behavior.

Housing Leaf-Tailed Geckos

Leaf-tailed geckos do best in a vertically oriented tropical vivarium, as described in Chapter 3. The basic requirements are plants, a tall glass vivarium (which helps retain humidity), and good lighting. For small species, such as *Uroplatus ebenaui* and *U. phantasticus*, the vivarium should be a minimum of 20 gallons (76 L). If housing multiple specimens together (two males may be kept together), pro-

This Henkel's leaf-tailed gecko specimen (*Uroplatus henkeli*) may be showing an atypical pattern because it is under stress; usually this species is brown and gray. It also has a huge mouth and may be a foot in length.

vide a vivarium at least 21 inches (53 cm) tall to have more territory for each gecko. A vivarium that includes a top screen lid and side door is very convenient for access. For large species, such as *U. henkeli* and *U. lineatus*, the vivarium should be a minimum of 45 gallons (170 L); hexagonal tanks are quite popular because of their great depth and height. Vivaria made entirely of screen do not work well with *Uroplatus* because the geckos in this genus need the high humidity a glass vivarium affords. In addition, the large branches needed by larger leaf-tails are not easy to anchor securely in a screen vivarium.

Uroplatus geckos often sit on sturdy plants such as *Sansevieria*, hide in philodendron, and use small weeping figs, *Ficus benjamina*. Smaller species appreciate dense plantings. Bamboo or PVC pipe sections slightly larger in diameter than the geckos are excellent. At least one piece should be oriented diagonally and another piece horizontally if possible. Leaf-tails will use many types of natural or artificial branches as resting places and especially favor branches with lichens and mosses on them.

For the substrate, use 2 to 3 inches (5 to 7.5 cm) of mulch topped by orchid bark of appropriate size for the species. Since these geckos are arboreal, they seldom come to the ground except to lay eggs, but the substrate helps increase the humidity in the vivarium.

A basking lamp is only necessary if the room where the geckos are being kept falls below a normal room temperature range of 70°F to 82°F (21°C to 28°C). In these cases, use a metal clamp-lamp with a household incandescent bulb of appropriate low wattage to provide a warm spot in the normal room temperature range. Do not overheat! Temperatures that exceed 95°F (35°C) can be fatal, even if the gecko is exposed for a short period. Keep the vivarium at mild room temperatures. Light does not seem critical to leaf-tail health. Full-spectrum reptile lights (with UV-A and UV-B) are OK but not necessary.

If your gecko's vivarium drops below 55°F (13°C) at night when the incandescent light is off, use a porcelain heat emitter (provides heat without light) to bring the temperature up. Remember that *Uroplatus* need complete darkness at night (Svatek and van Duin 2001). Use a spray bottle or a more elaborate misting system as the water source. *Uroplatus* species need to be misted once or more daily depending on the humidity requirements of the species. Be sure to mist at least once at night, preferably right after the vivarium lights switch off. Leaf-tails prefer to drink droplets of water from plant leaves and off the sides of the vivarium, although they will drink out of a water dish. A clean water dish should always be available.

Be aware that most *Uroplatus* specimens available in the pet trade today are wild-caught and may carry parasites. If this is the case with your gecko, use a simple vivarium setup and quarantine procedures as discussed in chapter 5. Always choose captive-bred specimens if possible!

Feeding Leaf-Tailed Geckos

Leaf-tailed geckos are insectivorous to carnivorous. The diet should be as varied as possible. Make sure that food items are no larger than the gecko's head. Crickets provide the bulk of the diet. Large species eat roughly ½-inch (1.2-cm) and larger crickets, and small species eat ½-inch (1.2-cm) and smaller crickets. Feed adults three or four times weekly, ten to twelve crickets per feeding. Feedings may be increased in frequency in warmer weather or decreased in cooler weather; adjust the feeding schedule to suit the gecko's appetite.

Mealworms and waxworms (as an occasional treat only due to their high fat content) are fine for all adult leaf-tails. Superworms can be a great snack food for large species only. Snails, if you can find cultured species (wild ones may be contaminated with herbicides and pesticides), are a delicacy these geckos crave; they are a good source of calcium and are beneficial for breeding females.

Your pet also will appreciate cultured cockroaches (those that are available commercially, which are uncontaminated with pesticides). Clean, preferably cultured, moths and flies are a good food as well.

A good supplementation regimen is T-Rex Leopard Gecko Dust ICB (Insect Cricket Balancer) at every feeding plus Miner-All (with vitamin D_3) once or twice per week (Neil Meister, pers. comm.). Females especially need calcium separately, in a small dish or as weekly liquid calcium drops, so they produce fertile eggs and can avoid hypocalcemia.

Breeding Leaf-Tailed Geckos

Sexing *Uroplatus* specimens is a simple matter due to the easily visible round hemipenal bulges in males, and their absence in females. *U. phantasticus* and *U. ebenaui* males may also have serrations on their tails (but not always, so be cautious). Males are tolerant of other males, so it is possible

Notice the fringes of skin on the jaws and sides of this Henkel's leaf-tailed gecko (*Uroplatus henkeli*). These fringes help camouflage the lizard by softening the outlines of the body and helping the gecko blend into the background.

to have more than one male in a breeding setup. Both sexes of leaf-tails are sexually mature in about one year. A pair will start breeding in spring, and egg-laying will taper as autumn approaches.

Egg Management

Look for eggs about thirty days after the first breeding. Two hard-shelled eggs will be laid in a clutch and buried in substrate or placed in plants. Put the eggs in a separate container such as a clear, plastic deli cup with a lid and air holes for ventilation. The eggs should be incubated at 80 to 100 percent relative humidity. To maintain this humidity, put approximately 2 inches (5 cm) of moist vermiculite, perlite, or sphagnum moss in the bottom of the deli cup, with the eggs sitting in a bottle cap on top. Check the substrate regularly to make sure it is moist enough (moist to the touch is a good general indicator). *Uroplatus* species may be safely incubated at about 80°F to 82°F (27°C to 28°C). A nighttime temperature drop of about ten degrees Fahrenheit (roughly six degrees Celsius) results in increased vitality in hatchlings. Look for the babies to hatch in as early as fifty days in smaller species or in as long as seventy days or more in larger species.

Hatchling Management

Hatchling leaf-tails are simply smaller versions of their parents. They require smaller food items offered more frequently as well as more frequent misting. Because they are so small, they are at risk of dehydration, but this is easy to avoid with the proper vivarium setup. Transfer hatchlings of small species (*U. phantasticus, U. ebenaui*) by encouraging them to hop onto a strip of paper towel and then moving them on the paper towel. Do not handle hatchlings, as they are too small and delicate at this size. Those of larger species (*U. henkeli, U. lineatus*) are OK to pick up carefully to transfer them to their hatchling vivarium. Same species clutch mates may be housed together.

Feed hatchlings daily. Small species get five or six pinhead crickets to start, large species get five or six two-week-old crickets to start. Provide supplementation as for the adults. Use a bottle cap or a plastic lid as a water dish. Move the hatchlings into a small glass vivarium with a screen top (use the same setup as for adults, just smaller). Plastic critter boxes are also great for raising hatchlings, but be sure you maintain high humidity for them. Mist the sides of the container and plants at least twice daily.

Notes on Selected Species
Species of *Uroplatus* often are difficult to identify because there is a lot of individual variation and some different species look similar.

Henkel's Leaf-Tailed Gecko
Uroplatus henkeli
This is an intermediate species for keepers who have reptile experience.

This leaf-tailed gecko is almost indistinguishable against the ground. Rarely seen just a few years ago, leaf-tailed geckos now are moderately common in the vivarium though still best kept only by experienced hobbyists.

U. henkeli ranges from the northwestern to the southwestern part of Madagascar. It is found in lower trunk zones of tropical, deciduous dry forests on small-diameter trees near brooks and rivers.

One of the largest species of *Uroplatus*, this gecko has dermal fringes around the body, especially under the chin. The body is elongated, and the mouth is very large. Daytime coloration is much paler than nighttime coloration. The body shows various patterns of mottled browns along with fine spotting. Males have larger dark patches than females have. *U. henkeli* may be as much as 11²/₅ inches (29 cm) in total length.

U. henkeli is the most readily available captive-bred leaf-tailed gecko, is one of the easiest species to keep, and is the best to start with in the genus. A limited amount of handling is possible, keeping the gecko's comfort zone in mind. This gecko is physically strong, and you will find out quickly if it does not want to be picked up. (The gecko will bite and or try to escape with vigor!) Mist the vivarium at least once a day to achieve optimal humidity.

Nosy Be or Spear-Point Leaf-Tailed Gecko
Uroplatus ebenaui
This species is for the advanced keeper with gecko experience.

This Nosy Be leaf-tailed geckos (*Uroplatus ebenaui*) perches high on a branch. Unlike many other leaf-tailed geckos, this gecko has few skin fringes on the body, and the sides of the sharply pointed tail are not notched.

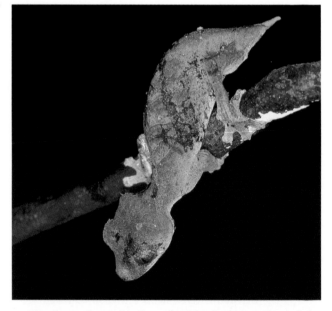

Uroplatus ebenaui is from the island of Nosy Be and the mainland of northwestern Madagascar, where it occurs in the lower scrub layer of tropical deciduous dry forests.

This is a small gecko that looks like a leaf, both in form and color. The tail is short and resembles a spear (thus the common name spear-point). The species comes in a variety of colors, from gold to red and black, and the body may have spots that resemble moss. The eyes are relatively large and the snout is short. *U. ebenaui* greatly resembles the larger *U. phantasticus*, but size and tail structure will distinguish them. At only 3¼ inches (8.3 cm) in total length, *U. ebenaui* is what hobbyists consider a micro-gecko.

U. ebenaui, the smallest leaf-tailed gecko, is frequently hard to find in the vivarium during the day if the enclosure is densely planted. This species is a legendary twig, leaf, and branch mimic! *U. ebenaui* enjoys leaf litter on the bottom of the vivarium—this material can be placed on top of orchid bark substrate. This small species has a very gentle disposition and is only aggressive toward food. This gecko is delicate and does not tolerate handling well. A well-cared-for specimen will provide lots of entertainment for the keeper as the animal hunts food during the evening hours. Adequate humidity can be achieved by misting twice daily and once at night. This gecko is considered difficult to breed successfully, and captive management is complex due to the gecko's small size and specific requirements for setup and maintenance.

Satanic Leaf-Tailed Gecko
Uroplatus phantasticus
This is an advanced species requiring gecko experience.

Satanic leaf-tailed geckos (*Uroplatus phantasticus*) are among the strangest geckos. They have a variety of small fringes and spines on the body and deep notches in the tail to mimic a dead leaf.

U. phantasticus live in tropical evergreen and deciduous transitional forests in northern to eastern central and southeastern coastal areas of Madagascar.

This small leaf-tail looks a lot like *U. ebenaui*. Like the Nosy Be (spear-point) gecko, the satanic leaf-tail's body shape and color mimic the leaves and twigs it lives among in its natural habitat. (There is, however, much variation among populations in color and pattern.) Its tail looks like a leaf in contrast to *U. ebenaui*, whose tail looks like a spear. *U. phantasticus* is a bit longer than *U. ebenaui*, up to 4½ inches (11 cm) in total length.

On more than one occasion, I have observed these leaf-tails hanging head-downward, grasping a branch with a foot or two, and curling up their tails—apparently normal behavior for this species. Management is the same as it is for *U. ebenaui*.

Lined Leaf-Tailed or Lined Flat-Tailed Gecko
Uroplatus lineatus

An intermediate species requiring some reptile experience.

U. lineatus comes from coastal tropical rain forests of northeastern Madagascar, including the coastal island of Nosy Boraha. It lives in a rainy, humid climate, where

Unlike most other leaf-tailed geckos (*Uroplatus lineatus*), the lined leaf-tail is partial to bamboo thickets, where the striped pattern helps it disappear among the vertical bamboo stems.

it occurs in the central vegetation layers of evergreen tropical forests and transitional deciduous forests. It prefers bamboo thickets.

One of the largest species of *Uroplatus*, it is slender with various darker and lighter stripes (*lineatus* means striped in Latin). Daytime coloration is much paler than nighttime coloration. It has a single pointed scale ("eyelash") above each eye. Females have two prominent white dashed lines running down the length of the body, whereas males have a single mottled white stripe. *U. lineatus* commonly is 10 to 11 inches (25 to 28 cm) long.

Management is similar to *U. henkeli*. Since *U. lineatus* prefers bamboo, be sure to put some in the vivarium. It has been bred with good success in captivity. The eggs are fragile and may occasionally stick to objects in the vivarium. Some specimens may be aggressive toward handling attempts, so proceed with caution when first handling a new pet.

Madagascan Ground Geckos
Genus *Paroedura*

Madagascan ground geckos belong to the genus *Paroedura* and occur mostly on the large island of Madagascar, though some of the fifteen known species are found on Indian Ocean islands as far away as the Comoros. Many of *Paroedura*'s species are extremely rare and have restricted ranges. Only a few species are found widely in the pet trade.

Paroedura species are nocturnal geckos that have adhesive lamellae (pads) on the toes, allowing them to climb up tree trunks and rock cliffs in their natural environment. Many species are almost completely arboreal, living in trees and resting with the head pointing downward in the same manner as *Uroplatus* species. However, our two most commonly available species, *P. androyensis* and *P. picta*, are almost exclusively terrestrial. As a rule, *Paroedura* geckos do not like to be handled, and the larger species may inflict a painful bite. This genus is made up of active predators, making them great choices if you like to observe hunting and eating in the vivarium.

Housing

Our chosen *Paroedura* of interest, *P. androyensis* and *P. picta*, are terrestrial geckos best suited to a horizontally oriented vivarium. Glass vivaria are best for creating attractive gecko displays in the home. As a low budget option, clear or opaque plastic storage containers with quarter-inch (6-mm) air holes drilled for adequate ventilation may be used. Make sure the top fits tightly to prevent escapes. A vivarium of 5 to 10 gallons (19 to 38 L) works well for housing up to five *P. androyensis*; a 10 to 20 gallon (38 to 76 L) will work for up to five *P. picta*. Vivaria that have sliding screen tops are a bit more expensive, but they are convenient for supporting basking lights and keeping out predators, such as cats. Be aware that small specimens of either species may climb up glass and escape through small gaps.

The Madagascan ground gecko (*Paroedura picta*) is a small, very prolific terrestrial gecko, easily kept and bred but usually short lived. Over the years, it has acquired many other common names, including big-headed gecko and ocelot gecko.

During the day, maintain temperatures between 77°F and 84°F (25°C and 29°C) for *P. androyensis*, and between 77°F and 88°F (25°C to 31°C) for *P. picta*. Do not overheat because temperatures above the recommended range can be fatal. Temperatures should not go below 65°F (18°C) at night for either species. If needed to maintain nighttime temperature, use a 25-watt incandescent bulb in a clamp-light, a porcelain infrared light, or an undertank heater. A red or blue 25-watt incandescent bulb should maintain the temperature above 65°F (18°C), and it will allow you to observe your gecko at night. Full-spectrum reptile lights are not necessary. Use a timer to turn the lights on and off with the same pattern as the sun.

The geckos will climb on small, artificial plants as well as on rocks and lengths of driftwood. Provide at least two hiding places for your geckos—one hiding place in the cool end of the vivarium, the other in the warm end. Preformed shelters from the pet store are great, but simple, cardboard paper towel rolls will suffice. The substrate should be 70 percent sphagnum moss and 30 percent sand to provide adequate relative humidity (70 to 80 percent). Cypress mulch also holds lots of humidity, but for *P. picta*, mix in some sand. Spray the sides of the vivarium with water daily, as well as the substrate to prevent it from drying out completely. Provide the usual water and food dishes.

Feeding

Paroedura are insectivores that need a varied diet. Larger species, such as *P. picta*, eat three-week-old (³/₈-inch, 10-mm) crickets. Small species, such as *P. androyensis*, eat two-week-old (¹/₄-inch, 6-mm) crickets. Feed adults three or four times weekly, eight to ten crickets per feeding. Feedings may be increased in frequency in warm weather or decreased in cool. Adjust the feeding schedule to suit the gecko's appetite.

Other suitable foods include mealworms for large species and miniature mealworms for small ones. Place them in a dish shallow enough for geckos to get into, and put a bit of powdered supplement in the bottom to brush off onto the larvae. Put fresh worms in every day. Waxworms are a great snack food for large species of *Paroedura*.

Give a good grade of reptile calcium and vitamin supplement, following label instructions; T-Rex Leopard Gecko ICB Dust works well. To avoid hypocalcemia and produce fertile eggs, females should be given additional calcium powder in a separate small dish. This point cannot be emphasized enough with *Paroedura* species because females tend to be prolific egg-layers and can crash quickly due to hypocalcemia if supplementation is not adequate. Watch for hypocalcemia symptoms of calcium tetany (twitching) and egg-binding. (See chapter 5 for more information on hypocalcemia.)

Breeding

The species of *Paroedura* discussed here sexually mature at six to seven months on average. Sex is easily determined by the presence of inflated hemipenial bulges in the male and their absence in females. As with other geckos, females should look stout and healthy before breeding. Breeding normally occurs in the warmer months of the year. For the best success, keep sexual pairs or trios together. Two hard-shelled fragile eggs, usually buried in the substrate, are laid about thirty days after mating. Eggs are visible through the abdominal skin of the female a few days before laying occurs.

Egg Management

Eggs should be collected and incubated separately from the parents, as the adults may eat the eggs or hatchlings. (Cannibalism is especially prevalent among calcium-deprived females.) A little careful digging is usually necessary to recover the fragile eggs. Put the eggs in a bottle cap in a separate container, such as a clear plastic deli cup with a lid and air holes. In some cases, eggs will be stuck to objects in the vivarium or to the vivarium itself. Do not attempt to pry off stuck eggs, as they will break with surprisingly little force. Isolate the stuck eggs from the parents. Put a plastic medicine cup (with a few air holes) or some sterile medical gauze over the eggs, and secure the protective cover with tape. This method allows the eggs to breathe and allows you to monitor their status while they're housed in the protective cover. Once the babies hatch, collect them and set them up in a separate container.

Eggs should be incubated in the 80°F to 84°F (27°C to 29°C) temperature range and at about 70 percent relative humidity for *P. picta*, 80 percent relative humidity for *P. androyensis*. You don't need a special incubator; just keep the cup in an area that maintains the correct temperature and humidity. Use a hygrometer to measure the humidity accurately. Using about 2 inches (5 cm) of moist vermiculite, perlite, or sphagnum moss in the bottom of the cup should provide enough moisture. Check the substrate

A Madagascan ground gecko begins to emerge from its egg. Both the egg shells and hatchlings are delicate and should never be handled directly.

regularly to make sure it does not dry out. Look for the babies to hatch as early as forty-five days (smaller species) or as long as seventy days (larger species). As incubation temperature increases, time to hatching decreases.

Hatchling Management

Transfer *P. androyensis* hatchlings by encouraging them to hop onto a strip of paper towel and then carrying them on the paper towel. Do not handle them, as they are too small and delicate at this size. House the hatchlings in a clear 16-ounce (0.47-L) deli cup or similar container. Clutch mates can be kept together in larger plastic containers with small air holes—a container with at least a 6-inch (15-cm) diameter and 2-inch (5-cm) depth will suffice (available commercially at reptile packaging dealers). Place a few strips of paper towel inside to create a place for the geckos to sit and hide. If space allows, put in half a toilet paper roll as a shelter and cover it with paper towel strips. Mist the sides of the container (not the paper towel) once daily so the young geckos will get a drink and proper humidity at the same time. Change the towels and container frequently to keep things clean. Keep under regular room lighting (no special lighting is needed for this nocturnal species unless needed for a heat source) and between 77°F and 84°F (25°C and 29°C) during daylight hours. At night, the lights should be turned off and temperatures kept above 65°F (18°C). Feed daily on three to five pinhead crickets to start. When the hatchlings graduate to week-old crickets and miniature mealworms, you can move the young geckos into a small glass vivarium with a screen top setup, much as for adults. The screen must be fine enough to prevent escapes, especially for this sticky-footed gecko, which can scale the vivarium walls and will easily find slits in the screening. A small number of juveniles can be housed together in this setup as long as they don't fight and they are all similar in size. Provide the usual calcium and vitamin supplements.

P. picta hatchlings also should not be handled directly. These young can be moved by carefully coaxing the geckos into a plastic cup or net, then relocating them to a small glass vivarium or plastic container as described above. Small plastic critter boxes are also great for raising hatchlings. Keep them either in pairs or individually. Remove larger or aggressive clutch mates. Feed week-old crickets to start; graduate to two-week-old crickets in two or three weeks. Small mealworms and similar insects are accepted. Mist the sides of the container and the hatchlings daily.

Notes on Selected Species
In addition to the following two species, *Paroedura bastardi*, which is very similar to *P. picta*, sometimes is kept.

Small Madagascan Ground Gecko
Paroedura androyensis
Due to the small size of this species, only the advanced keeper with gecko experience should try to keep this gecko.

This terrestrial species is found in Madagascar along the eastern coast to the southern tip. It lives in deciduous dry forests in leaf litter in southern locations and on the floor of the tropical rain forest on the eastern coast.

P. androyensis is a very small gecko with primarily brown coloration that varies in shade in different specimens. Dorsal patterns are extremely variable. The belly is white. Scalation is very fine and soft to the touch, the eyes are gold over the top quarter and then brown. The snout is short. The tail stores fat and is covered with soft

Less than 3 inches long, the small Madagascan ground gecko (*Paroedura androyensis*) is considered a micro-gecko.

tuberculate scales that are white to brown in color; the tail can be regenerated if broken off. Hatchlings have bright orange tails. Hobbyists consider *P. androyensis* one of the micro-geckos; adults may be only 2 ²/₅ inches (6 cm) in total length.

P. androyensis are perhaps the most sought-after micro-geckos because their coloration and patterns are extremely beautiful. During the day, they sleep in the curl of a leaf or under a hide box. Pieces of cork bark work well for this species as places to climb and hide. At night, they get on the highest point in the vivarium, such as a rock or hide box, and wave their tails back and forth. This behavior is most likely intended to distract prey before the gecko snaps up its dinner, or it may be a territorial, defensive, or courtship display. Any combination of males and females that are about the same in size seem compatible in appropriate-size vivaria.

Remove eggs immediately—this little gecko definitely will eat its offspring! Eggs are usually laid under hide boxes and other objects in the vivarium. Be extremely careful picking up the eggs as they very fragile. Even hatchlings can lose their tails, though they usually survive this misfortune and regenerate their tails.

Madagascan Ground Gecko
Paroedura picta
This is an intermediate species requiring gecko experience.

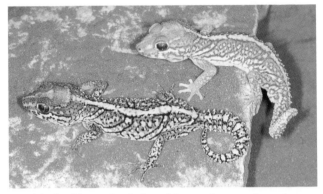

Here are two different morphs of the Madagascan ground gecko (*Paroedura picta*). The gecko at the top is an albino (xanthic), lacking the black pigment, while the more normally patterned one has an exceptionally distinct stripe down the back.

This familiar gecko is found in southern and southwestern Madagascar in dry desert and savannah regions. During the day it hides under rocks and in shallow burrows. At night it can be seen running along the sand.

P. picta (the species name was formerly spelled *pictus*) is a medium-size gecko with a big head and powerful jaws. Many different color morphs and patterns occur, the most common being banded or striped. Basic coloration is cream with broad brown bands or patches edged with black, much as in young leopard geckos. The belly is white. Juveniles usually have sharply banded or striped patterns that break up into adult patterns as they age. The tail can store a small amount of fat and will regenerate if lost. *P. picta* may be $5\frac{1}{2}$ inches (14 cm) long.

P. picta is readily available in captive-bred form, perhaps the most commonly available captive-bred Madagascan gecko. This is a good second gecko after one has had either a leopard or crested gecko. In its natural habitat, this gecko spends its days hiding in moist places and its nights foraging in the sand. An enclosure of 10 gallons (38 L) or more will allow you to create two areas to simulate the natural environment: a humid side, accomplished by including a peat moss and sand mix substrate, and a dry, sandy area. *P. picta* males do not get along. Once the geckos are sexually mature, be sure to keep only one male in a group.

This gecko is easy to breed. Males are slightly larger than females. Some males are aggressive breeders and may have to be removed to protect the females.

CHAPTER 9

TOKAY GECKOS AND RELATED SPECIES

Tokay geckos (*Gekko gecko*) were one of the first species described that now are placed in the family Gekkonidae, the geckos proper or true geckos. Most authorities place all but the eyelid geckos, the eublepharids, in Gekkonidae, though some now think that Gekkonidae should be split on the basis of relatively small differences in the skull and the skeleton. In this chapter, we will focus on just a few species of the genus *Gekko*. Note that the generic name is spelled differently from the common name—*gekko* versus *gecko*.

Tokay geckos (*Gekko gecko*) are big, beautiful lizards with definite personalities. They should be handled with care because you can tear their skin—and they can bite hard.

Many species of *Gekko* fail to attract keepers with their plain shades of brown and indistinct patterns. The three species covered in this chapter, however, have attractive colors or patterns. These are the hardy and familiar tokay gecko (*Gekko gecko*), the golden gecko (*G. ulikovskii*), and the white-lined gecko (*G. vittatus*). They all are large species, commonly 7 to 10 inches (18 to 25 cm).

These large, tropical Asian geckos are nocturnal and arboreal. They have sticky feet, with wide pads under the toes, and claws. Most are commonly available as wild-caught specimens in the pet trade (though some captive-bred specimens are sold). As wild-caught geckos, they tend to be aggressive and nippy, especially the tokay, which can inflict a very painful bite in keeping with its large size. If acquired as wild-caught specimens, they will need to be kept in quarantine (see chapter 5) and will likely need to be treated for both mites and intestinal parasites. Wild-caught specimens should be moved with a bird net, and handling should be avoided; they will drop the tail when trapped. As with any reptile, it is preferable to obtain these species as captive-bred specimens, but there is more than just a health advantage in this case because captive-breds are much more docile in temperament than their wild-caught counterparts.

Tokay geckos are noted for their vocalizations, which sound like their name, *toe-kay*, at least to some observers.

The toe tips of tokay geckos are very wide and covered with rows of adhesive lamellae and millions of microscopic hairs that let the pads serve as suction cups and make these geckos strong climbers.

All three species will produce soft to loud "chuck" and "click" sounds at night, but the tokay can really sound off.

Housing

Our three species of *Gekko* are all tropical geckos that can live in the same type of vivarium as used for the largest day geckos, so refer to chapter 7 for basic vivarium setup notes. The exception is that you must start with at least a 20-gallon (76-L) tall vivarium for an adult pair of tokays. A 45-gallon (170-L) hexagonal vivarium works well with these species and is a good size for a breeding trio of one male and two females. Basking spots should not exceed 84°F (29°C) during the day, and the temperature of the enclosure should not drop below 65°F (18°C) at night. Tokays differ from day geckos in that they are mostly active at night (though often they will come out of hiding in an upper corner of the vivarium to eat during the day) and have a thicker skin that allows them to survive in drier conditions.

Keepers prefer gecko species with interesting color patterns, such as the white-lined gecko (*Gekko vittatus*), rather than the more common brown color species.

Feeding

The feeding regime is also similar to that of large day geckos, except that these *Gekko* species are primarily insectivorous and can eat larger, fully grown crickets (up to seven weeks old), pinky mice, and even cockroaches more than an inch (2.5 cm) long (a favorite food in the wild). A typical feeding schedule is three to four times weekly, at least ten crickets per feeding.

Breeding

Once you have established a pair or trio and they are healthy, they will breed and lay eggs. You may hear vocalizations during the courting and mating process, which is a sign that the lizards are well established.

Egg Management

The hard-shelled eggs of these geckos are usually stuck together and glued, in the same fashion as those of day geckos, to solid surfaces, such as cork bark or the vivarium glass. Do not attempt to move the eggs from where they are attached as they will break easily. Instead, protect the eggs with a clear plastic deli cup of the appropriate size, punched with air holes and taped over the eggs. This will protect them from accidental damage and the hatchlings from adult predation. Tokays are known to guard their eggs and offspring and may bite, so be careful when tending to eggs in the vivarium. Look for eggs about thirty days after the first mating.

Caution!

Tokay and other hard-shelled gecko eggs are not forgiving of rough treatment, so take care in their removal and handling.

If you are able to collect the eggs (for instance, if they are attached to a leaf or bit of bark that can be cut off and moved), put them in a small bottle cap that is then placed in a container, such as a clear plastic deli cup with a lid and air holes punched to allow ventilation. Eggs should be incubated at about 70 percent relative humidity; use a hygrometer to measure humidity. The most common way to achieve the necessary humidity is to use approximately 2 inches (5 cm) of moist vermiculite, perlite, or sphagnum moss at the bottom of the container and place the eggs in the bottle cap on top. Check the substrate periodically to make sure it remains moist enough. Err on the dry side as babies will drown in the egg from excessive water absorption if the substrate is too moist. Incubate the eggs at roughly 80°F to 84°F (27°C to 29°C). All that is needed is the correct temperature range and humidity, not a fancy incubator. Try to find a suitable place in your home to keep the eggs during their incubation period—perhaps on a warm shelf or in the gecko's vivarium. Look for the babies to hatch in as little as sixty-five days or as long as two hundred days.

Hatchling Management
Hatchling management is the same as for large *Phelsuma* species (see chapter 7). However, hatchlings need to be kept in 5-gallon (19-L) vivaria or larger because they hatch at about 4 inches (10 cm) in length in the larger species.

Notes on Selected Species
Though several species of tokays (a name given in general to the genus *Gekko*) are known from southern Asia, only three species appear with regularity in the pet shops and are widely kept.

Tokay Gecko
Gekko gecko
This is an intermediate species that requires some previous gecko experience.

A nicely marked tokay gecko (*Gekko gecko*) displays a varied pattern of rusty red and whitish spots on a distinctly bluish background.

The tokay gecko has a very wide range in southern Asia, where it is common from India and Bangladesh through Myanmar (formerly Burma) and Thailand, over Southeast Asia to most islands of Indonesia and the Philippines, as well as southern China. It has been introduced into Florida and Hawaii, as well as Martinique in the Caribbean. Though originally a species of tropical forests, it also adapts well to life in villages.

This is a large gecko that may have bright colors when healthy. It has a blue-gray background color sprinkled with many red spots. The body is heavy, the large head has muscular jaws, and the tail is quite long and slender. An adult tokay may weigh in at an impressive $3\,^1/_2$ to $5\,^1/_4$ ounces (100 to 150 grams), with large males weighing as much as $10\,^1/_2$ ounces (300 g). *Gekko gecko* is long, at 8 to 10 inches (20 to 25 cm) in adult females and 12 to 14 inches (30 to 36 cm) in adult males.

The tokay is one of the best display geckos a hobbyist could hope to obtain. It has a loud voice and is considered good luck in its native range. (Tokays are appreciated for their eating of insects in people's homes.) Tragically, this gecko is also exploited to make aphrodisiacs and other native medicines. It has many interesting behaviors that make it a great gecko for the hobbyist, but it is aggressive if wild-caught and should be handled with a soft net if it is necessary to move it. Captive-bred specimens are highly desirable and can be located with research. Sexing is relatively easy, as males are larger than females and have very pronounced femoral pores. Take extra care to make sure you do not put two males together—they will fight, and in this very aggressive species, the males could easily injure each other.

Golden Gecko
Gekko ulikovskii

This is species is best for the intermediate keeper with some reptile experience.

This gecko was described only a few years ago and so far has only been found in Vietnam. Though it primarily lives in tropical forests, it also lives in villages.

The golden gecko is similar in general appearance to the tokay, though it is a bit more slender with a less massive head. Its long body is dull greenish tan with a distinctive yellowish tinge over most of the back. *G. ulikovskii* is smaller than *G. gecko*, usually just 6 to 7 inches (15 to 18 cm) long.

Golden geckos (*Gekko ulikovskii*) were described only a few years ago and are better known in the vivarium than in nature. A healthy specimen has a unique golden green glow and very soft skin.

Typically, golden geckos are not as aggressive as tokays and may be handled to some degree, though they often are shyer and the skin may be more delicate. Introduce handling slowly. Management and breeding are much the same as for *G. gecko*.

White-Lined Gecko
Gekko vittatus

This species is recommended for the intermediate keeper, requiring some reptile experience.

This distinctive species is typically imported from Indonesia (especially Java and Timor) and New Guinea and occurs widely over the larger islands of Oceania, including Belau, the Admiralty Islands, and the Bismarck Archipelago and Solomon Islands. It lives in tropical forests as well as near and in human-modified habitats.

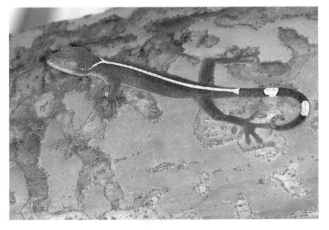

The distinctive stripe running down the center of its back has earned the white-lined gecko (*Gekko vittatus*) another name—skunk gecko.

A large, slender green or brownish gecko, it is immediately recognizable because of the white stripe running down its back—a characteristic that lends to its alternative common name, the skunk gecko. Large adults may be 8 to 10 inches (20 to 25 cm) long.

The white-lined gecko is mild mannered compared with *G. gecko*. Sometimes it may curl its tail if disturbed. Some handling may be tolerated, but start it slowly. Care and breeding are much the same as for *G. gecko*.

CHAPTER 10

CRESTED GECKOS AND OTHER NEW CALEDONIANS

New Caledonian geckos of major interest to hobbyists are from the genus *Rhacodactylus*, often called the giant geckos. Currently, the following three species are widely sold and are considered in this chapter: the crested gecko (*Rhacodactylus ciliatus*); the gargoyle gecko (*R. auriculatus*); and the giant gecko (*R. leachianus*). There are two recognized subspecies of *R. leachianus*: the Grande Terre giant (*R. leachianus leachianus*) and Henkel's giant (*R. leachianus henkeli*). However, some herpetological opinions argue that *R. leachianus henkeli* may include at least two different types; several

In just a few years, the crested gecko (*Rhacodactylus ciliatus*) went from a virtually unknown and possibly extinct species to one of the most popular larger geckos in the vivarium hobby.

populations have been found living in specific types of environments that are physically distinctive (de Vosjoli, Fast, and Repashy 2003). Clearly, the taxonomy of this gecko needs more investigation, both scientifically and geographically, as certain islands have not been investigated.

All six species of *Rhacodactylus* come from the New Caledonian island chain located in the southern Pacific Ocean east of Australia and have their closest relatives on the Australian continent; the genus belongs to the subfamily Diplodactylinae, often considered a full family. All are quite large (body length 4 inches, 10 cm, or more), with relatively slender and often short tails. The toes have widened adhesive pads and claws, and the scales of the body are tiny. One species (*Rhacodactylus trachyrhynchus*) gives live birth. Though seven other genera of geckos are known from New Caledonia, the *Rhacodactylus* species are the only ones that reach the pet trade on a regular basis.

Rhacodactylus species are nocturnal, sleeping either in the open or in hiding places during the day. The three species covered in this chapter tolerate handling well, especially if handled regularly as juveniles. New Caledonian gecko keepers should not be surprised if their specimen's prehensile tail breaks off, usually due to aggression from cage mates, and does not regenerate fully. In the wild, New Caledonians are usually tailless, likely due to intraspecific (same species) aggression. New Caledonians are mostly arboreal, though the gargoyle gecko also spends a good deal of time on the ground. All *Rhacodactylus* species have adhesive lamellae that easily grip vertical surfaces, such as glass, and often the toes are connected by webs of skin.

Housing

In general, New Caledonians do well with a vertically oriented tropical vivarium similar to that used for large day geckos (genus *Phelsuma*). Glass vivaria with a screened side-opening door, in addition to a top screen opening, are preferred for ease of maintenance.

Display vivarium size for housing up to three crested geckos should be a minimum of 20 gallons (76 L). For a pair

A fairly typical New Caledonian giant gecko, the gargoyle gecko (*Rhacodactylus auriculatus*) also has been called the eared gecko because of small bones that project from the back of the head like a pair of ears.

of Grande Terre giant geckos, a $30 \times 10^{1}/_{2} \times 25^{1}/_{2}$ -inch ($76 \times 27 \times 65$ cm) glass vivarium with a sliding screen top and side door opening at one narrow end works well. For a pair of gargoyle geckos, the same style vivarium is recommended, but at a size of $21 \times 14^{1}/_{2} \times 14^{1}/_{2}$ -inch ($53 \times 37 \times 37$ cm).

Outdoor vivaria constructed of mostly screen may be used in mild climate that maintain 70 percent relative humidity or more and if you carefully monitor the temperature. The enclosure must be made of screen to avoid cooking the gecko in a glass cage that overheats. Direct sunlight will kill your gecko! You should also keep a watchful eye out for predators, such as ants and cats.

Rhacodactylus species will require plants in their vivaria. These lizards use plants for shelters and basking sites. Artificial plants will do, but several live plants are easy to keep and will add to the naturalistic setting you create for your pet. (Wedging potted plants into the substrate—as opposed to planting them directly into the ground medium—allows for easy removal if the plants need to be watered or replaced.) Some plants are used to sit on, like *Sansevieria* (mother in-law's tongue or snake plants), and others to hide behind, such as philodendrons and small weeping fig trees (*Ficus benjamina*). But do not clutter the vivarium with plants; leave a good portion of the vertical space open so these active geckos can move around. Consider adding bamboo sections or short lengths of PVC pipe slightly larger in diameter than the geckos. At least one piece should be diagonally oriented, with another piece horizontally oriented, if possible. These are important to avoid flop-tail syndrome (see chapter 3). Be sure that all vivarium decorations are sturdy and securely attached, especially in the case of the larger species (*R. leachianus*), whose body weight may not be supported by loosely arranged cage decorations.

Cork bark tubes and large pieces of cork bark are attractive and will be used as shelters. Include some ground-level shelters, such as plastic hide boxes. Make sure the shelters will not collapse on the gecko.

The substrate should consist of 2 to 3 inches (5 to 7.5 cm) of mulch topped by orchid bark of an appropriate size for the geckos (larger grade for larger species). As a low-budget option, you can use paper-towel tubes or sections of cage carpeting for substrate.

A common mistake made by beginners is overheating these geckos. Most novices assume all geckos are from hot tropical or desert climates; this is not true. Many geckos—and *Rhacodactylus* are some of these—are from climates with mild temperatures. Heat can be provided by a household incandescent bulb of about 25 watts, mostly to provide light in the vivarium for plants and a mild basking spot for the lizards. Increase wattage as needed to achieve average daytime room temperatures in the middle to upper seventies Farenheit (mid-twenties Celcius). (Daytime temperature can drop about ten degrees Fahrenheit, six degrees Celsius, in the winter months.) Screw the bulb into a metal cone or clamp-light at attach it to the screen top of the vivarium; choose a fixture with a diameter wide enough that the lamp doesn't easily topple off the cage top. Reptile full-spectrum UV-B tubes may be used but are not necessary if the geckos are healthy and given supplements in their food. Use a timer to turn lights on at sunrise, off at sundown. Maintain a nighttime temperature of at least 60°F (16°C); if needed, supply heat with an infrared heat emitter or a red or blue bulb when the main incandescent light is off.

New Caledonians need their vivarium misted once or twice daily to maintain a relative humidity of about 70 percent. You can use a spray bottle or more elaborate automatic misting system. Like day geckos, *Rhacodactylus* species like to drink droplets of water from plant leaves and the sides of the vivarium, but this is usually not enough to keep them hydrated. A water dish should always be available, and the dish should be kept clean.

Feeding

New Caledonian geckos are both insectivorous and frugivorous, some species preferring more fruit than insects and other species preferring more insects than fruit. For example, *R. auriculatus* likes to eat more crickets than does *R. ciliatus*. The long-snouted Grande Terre giant (*R. leachianus leachianus*) is thought to eat more insects than shorter-snouted counterparts, who generally eat more fruit than insects. *Rhacodactylus ciliatus* eagerly takes supplemented crickets, T-Rex Crested Gecko Diet (no supplement required), as well as fruit puree coated in supplement powder.

Feed adults three times weekly during the warmer months, twice (or less) during the winter months. Offering only fruit puree does not contribute to sufficient nutrition. For frugivorous species, provide one weekly feeding of about ten to twelve crickets (size of cricket should be just a bit smaller than the size of the gecko's maximum head width) and two weekly feedings of fruit puree or species-specific diet servings. Your gecko will help you determine the serving size for puree or species-specific diet. Start with a mayonnaise jar lid filled to the rim, but increase the size of the feeding if the gecko goes through that amount completely in less than a day. Ideally, a little bit of food will be left over. For insectivorous species, each feeding should consist of two weekly feedings of crickets and one weekly fruit puree or commercial diet serving. Alternatively, you may feed all these geckos T-Rex species-specific diets for all feedings, as it is a nutritionally complete supplement.

Breeding

New Caledonian geckos will breed during the warm season. As with most geckos, a temperature drop of about ten degrees Fahrenheit (about six degrees Celsius) during winter is thought to facilitate breeding in the spring. *Rhacodactylus ciliatus* and *R. auriculatus* are among the easiest geckos to breed. Both these species are prolific, annually producing about ten clutches of two eggs each. *R. leachianus* is not as prolific (just four to six clutches a year) and is harder to pair up successfully.

Be sure to determine the sex of the two geckos before attempting to set up any breeding arrangement. Two mature male *R. leachianus* will fight, usually to the death,

Though quite a handful, this specimen of the New Caledonian giant gecko (*Rhacodactylus leachianus*) is actually a baby. The very heavy legs and short tail are typical of most Rhacodactylus species.

especially if a female is present. *R. ciliatus* males are more tolerant of each other even with sexually mature females present, although they lose their tails more easily with this arrangement. The New Caledonians discussed in this chapter can be kept in pairs; *R. ciliatus* and *R. auriculatus* will even form harems. The geckos should be of breeding age and weight (different for each species).

Extra calcium supplementation is critical for females to survive the breeding process and remain healthy. In addition to supplementing their regular food items, put a dish of calcium with vitamin D_3 (Rep-Cal with D_3 works well) in the vivarium for each breeding female so she can take what she needs. If females suffer egg-binding or produce weak offspring with kinky tails, there was insufficient calcium in the female's diet.

Egg Management

Two white, soft-shelled eggs are laid in moist substrate or in laying boxes (such as large margarine tubs) with moist substrate such as sphagnum moss. Collect the eggs as soon as possible (or they'll dry out), and set them up in a moist substrate. A 50:50 mix of perlite and vermiculite can be used as follows: five to eight parts of water should be added to ten parts of the dry substrate mix by weight. The moist substrate should be about 2 inches (5 cm) deep. Bury the eggs halfway into the substrate. Use clear plastic tubs or deli cups (with air holes) that are 6 ¾ inches (17 cm) in diameter and 2½ inches deep (6.4 cm) in diameter. Incubation temperatures used vary by species, so refer to the following individual species accounts for specifics. Babies hatch between 60 and 140 days in *R. ciliatus,* between 45 and 70 days in *R. auriculatus,* and between 90 and 153 days in *R. leachianus.* These times depend on temperatures used, as higher temperatures tend to decrease the incubation period. All three species exhibit temperature-dependent sex determination. Higher relative temperatures will result in more males and earlier hatching, whereas lower relative temperatures produce more females and longer incubation periods.

Hatchling Management

Hatchling New Caledonians are managed similarly to hatchlings of large *Phelsuma* species. *R. ciliatus* and *R. auriculatus* may be kept singly or in clutch mate pairs. One gallon (3.8 L) plastic critter boxes make fine enclosures for these hatchlings. Include paper towel substrate and cardboard paper-towel rolls to climb on and hide in. *R. leachianus* babies may be kept singly in this size setup, but they are too aggressive to be grouped together. *R. ciliatus* may be raised in groups of twenty or more in larger vivaria. When keeping more than one hatchling in a vivarium, watch for developing size differences and fights resulting in tail loss and other problems. Separate any hatchlings or juveniles exhibiting these behaviors immediately or their victims may be eaten or injured.

Offer hatchlings the same food and supplementation as adults of the same species, but adjust the proportions to their size and feed daily. Make sure fresh water is always available in shallow containers, taking care to avoid accidental death from drowning.

This baby gargoyle gecko (*Rhacodactylus auriculatus*) displays the common striped pattern of its species. As more keepers breed this gecko, they are finding new color and pattern morphs.

Notes on Selected Species

New Caledonian geckos have increased in popularity every year they have existed in captivity for good reasons. They are beautiful and exhibit interesting behaviors. Captive-bred crested geckos are readily available through the pet trade, and one does not have to look very hard to find a captive-bred gargoyle gecko either. Both these geckos are very hardy and easy to keep. The giant gecko is a bit harder to find and more expensive but well worth it if you have the prerequisite reptile experience under your belt.

Gargoyle Gecko
Rhacodactylus auriculatus
This species is recommended for a novice who has some reptile experience.

Gargoyle geckos are found only on the southern third of Grande Terre Island, the largest island of New Caledonia. It lives in scrub habitat and along clearings in primary forests.

This is a robust species with coarser scalation than seen in *R. ciliatus*. The head has bony protuberances above the ears, thus inspiring their scientific name, *auriculatus*, referring to external ears. This species also comes in many color morphs, the most well-known being patternless, reticulated (most common), and striped. Adults may have a body length of up to 5 inches (12.7 cm) and would be about 8 inches (20 cm) in total length with a complete tail. They weigh approximately $1^1/_2$ ounces (40 g).

The gargoyle gecko is easy to keep in captivity. It is not as social with its own kind, however, which makes it a bit more complicated to keep. Gargoyle owners must be on the look-out for fighting before small specimens are hurt or, in the worst case scenario, eaten.

It is not unusual for tails to be missing in this species. Unlike the tails of *R. ciliatus*, the tails of *R. auriculatus* regenerate to some extent. Handle gargoyles in the same manner as cresteds.

The tail of this gargoyle gecko seems to be complete, which is not common in species of *Rhacodactylus*. Most specimens of almost all species tend to lose much or all of the tail early in life.

Gargoyle geckos are usually sexually mature at twelve to eighteen months old. De Vosjoli and colleagues have had success incubating eggs in a fluctuating temperature range of 60°F to 81°F (16°C to 27°C), which usually results in a majority of females. Higher temperatures will result in more males, but for safe incubation, do not exceed 84°F (29°C).

Crested Gecko
Rhacodactylus ciliatus
This is a great species for the novice who has no reptile experience.

The narrow, erect scales projecting over the eyes of *Rhacodactylus ciliatus* have earned it the common name eyelash gecko among some keepers. The common name of crested gecko refers to the triangle of pointed scales at the back of the head.

Most crested geckos in captivity originated on the Isle of Pines, New Caledonia, where they were long thought to have become extinct—until observed after a storm in 1994. They are also found in Kutomo (next to Isle of Pines), southern Grande Terre, and the Belep Islands (north of Grande Terre). This species is found in undisturbed primary forest with a dense canopy.

The defining feature of this remarkable gecko is the presence of lateral crests running from the eyes, over the neck, and onto the back. These crests are sometimes referred to as eyelashes, influencing the crested gecko's alternative name, the eyelash gecko. The head is triangular, the body is stout, and the feet have adhesive pads and claws for climbing. The tail is prehensile, but in the wild most specimens lack tails, which do not regenerate. The skin of *R. ciliatus* is very soft to the touch because of the fine scalation. Typical crested geckos have a body length of 4 to 4 ³/₄ inches (10 to 11.9 cm) and a total length (with fully developed tail) of about 8 inches (20 cm). Adults typically weigh between 1 and 2 ounces (35 and 60 grams).

Though not as extensive as the pattern and color morphs of the leopard gecko, many morphs of captive-bred crested geckos exist, and new morphs regularly appear in the pet trade. Apparently, R. ciliatus develops distinctive, striking traits within just a few captive generations. Some of the current morphs are:

- Bicolor: two colored, high contrast (rare)
- Chevron-back: mostly patternless with cream yellow colored chevrons running down back
- Dalmatian: a speckled morph
- Fire or flame: a light dorsal color set off from the main body's darker hues by the crests
- Patternless: mostly uniform in color
- Pinstripe: a fire or harlequin (which is a fire morph with mottled pattern) morph that displays thin, white lines that run the length of the body
- Tiger: light background color streaked with high contrast pattern of a darker shade
- White-fringed: white lining on inner thigh area and often on the tail base and shins

Crested gecko morphs can involve more than color and pattern variations. Some morphs are structural, referring to variations in head size or width, and either presence or absence of the crest or eyelash scales. For example, crested geckos with typical broad-based-size heads are called normal; those with significantly more head width than length and unusually large crests are called crowned; and those with considerably more head length than width and reduced crests are called reverted. Reverted morphs are considered undesirable and should be culled out of breeding colonies.

R. ciliatus is an excellent starter gecko due to the simplicity of its care. It does, however, take a bit of patience for a novice to get used to handling these geckos because they like to hop when you first pick them up. When first picking up R. ciliatus, let the gecko run over your hands, one after another, until they settle down. This is called hand-walking.

Crested geckos can be sexed when just a few months old by looking for the presence or absence of inflated hemipenial pouches just behind the vent. *R. ciliatus* becomes sexually mature between one and two years of age. Females should not be bred until they have reached approximately an ounce (30 to 35 grams) in weight. Crested gecko eggs can be successfully incubated between 68°F and 84°F (20°C and 29°C), with an ideal temperature between 76°F and 78°F (24.5°C and 25.5°C).

The Giant Geckos

These geckos are recommended for the intermediate keeper with reptile experience.

The New Caledonian giant gecko (*Rhacodactylus leachianus*) is not only the longest gecko living today (reaching at least 13 inches) but also one of the bulkiest in build.

Giant geckos (*R. leachianus*) are restricted to New Caledonia and occur as two subspecies, both found in the hobby. The Grande Terre giant (*R. leachianus leachianus*) comes from Grande Terre Island, where it lives in primary forests of large trees with hollows; it needs access to the canopy and a diversity of trees, especially fruit trees. Henkel's giant (*R. leachianus henkeli*) comes from the Isle of Pines and neighboring islands, where it lives in different types of habitat from primary forests with 50-foot (15-m) trees to mixed forests and dry forests with low vegetation.

The Grande Terre giant is believed to be the largest gecko alive today, reaching a up to 13 inches (33 cm) long for the main body, with a total length (including the tail) about 17 inches (43 cm). The largest size morph can weigh up to 1 pound (454 g). Grande Terre females are usually heavier and longer than males. Henkel's giant is smaller, with a shorter tail. Body length varies among Henkel's giant populations, ranging from 5½ inches (14 cm) to 8 inches (21 cm). In this subspecies, males and females are about the same size. Due to the size, you should exercise caution when getting to know a new specimen, as it can inflict a very painful bite. In both forms, the tails regenerate if lost. These geckos, especially the Grande Terre form, are also known for their vocalizations.

Both Grande Terre and Henkel's giants come in a number of morphs and different body types, depending on the region they come from. The color morphs are usually either darker or lighter than the standard type and may have spotting or different degrees of mottling. (See de Vosjoli, Fast, and Repashy 2003, for specific information.)

Be sure you know the sex of the giant gecko before placing two geckos together to breed. Definitely do not keep any males together! Pairing is a delicate process. Watch new pairs for any signs of incompatibility (missing tails or other injuries, one sitting on the ground constantly); if you see such signs, remove one of the geckos immediately, as death can occur swiftly in this dangerous situation. Females may fight with each other after sexual maturity, so keep a very close eye on any giant geckos kept together. In the wild, opposite sex pairs frequent hollows of trees together; harems are not known to occur.

As with most geckos, the presence (male) or absence (female) of hemipenal bulges is the most obvious indicator of sex. These bulges can be seen in older juvenile and adult specimens. Generally, giant gecko males also tend to have thicker heads and bodies than females. Weight rather than age is a more reliable indicator of sexual maturity. *R. leachianus* females can take five or more years in the wild to become sexually mature. In captivity, however, this time can be shortened by increasing feeding schedules to reach breeding weight sooner. A female *R. leachianus* in her first year of sexual maturity may lay two clutches, in her later years an average of three clutches per year. A female's first clutch, as in many types of geckos, is often infertile. Eggs may be incubated in fluctuating temperatures between 68°F and 84°F (20°C and 29°C) and may hatch in 90 to 153 days, depending on whether the eggs have been incubated at lower or higher relative temperatures. Since size differentials frequently result in predation by the larger gecko, raise hatchlings singly.

CHAPTER 11

DESERT-DWELLING GECKOS

This chapter covers half a dozen genera of a physically diverse group of geckos that share a preference for dry, usually desert, habitats. They are relatively easy to care for due to the simplicity of their captive habitats, but few species have become widely available in pet shops because most are somewhat difficult to breed in captivity. All belong to the family Gekkonidae and usually are placed in the subfamily Gekkoninae, though some authorities would put the wonder geckos (genus *Teratoscincus*) into their own subfamily. Like other Gekkonidae members, these geckos lack eyelids.

Of these species, the helmeted gecko (*Geckonia chazaliae*), the viper gecko (*Teratolepis fasciata*), and the tiger or thick-toed gecko (*Pachydactylus tigrinus*) are considered micro-geckos by hobbyists due to their small size

The wonder gecko (*Teratoscincus scincus*) may be one of the oddest geckos around. It has exceptionally large eyes, and the body is covered with large, flat scales somewhat like those of a fish.

of 4 inches (10 cm) or less in length. The small, thin-bodied Namib sand or web-footed gecko (*Palmatogecko rangei*) would be the next largest at about 5 inches (12.7 cm) long. Next in size ranging between 4 and 6 inches (10 and 15 cm) long are the wonder geckos, *Teratoscincus scincus*, and their cousin, the heavier-bodied frog-eyed wonder gecko or Roborowski's gecko (*Teratoscincus roborowski*); and the Namib giant ground or giant sand gecko (*Chondrodactylus angulifer*). Female helmeted geckos, viper geckos, tiger (thick-toed) geckos, and Namib sand (web-footed) geckos are sexually dimorphic in that females are bigger than males, whereas male wonder geckos and the Namib giant ground gecko are typically slightly larger in size and have more massive heads than females, particularly in *C. angulifer*.

Both viper and helmeted geckos are docile, the best of our desert-dwellers for handling. The Namib sand gecko will tolerate some handling. As with any gecko species, be sure you stay within their comfort zone, immediately returning them to the vivarium if they show any signs of fear (vocalizations, backing away, or mouth gaping). The small size and delicate structure of the Namib sand gecko make handling problematic for all but the most experienced keepers. The Namib giant ground gecko should not be handled, as this species can inflict a painful bite and does not give much, if any, warning. The tiger gecko and both wonder gecko species dislike being handled, so only handle them if absolutely necessary. The tiger gecko is a nervous species that will readily drop its tail if you attempt to grasp it. The wonder geckos will "rattle" their scales when stressed and often shed scales if handled. These latter three geckos should be handled indirectly by carefully scooping them up into a plastic cup or by using a soft net. Hide boxes also work well as scoops.

Though generally nocturnal, all these geckos (except the tiger) are seen during the day, especially the Namib giant ground gecko, which has a huge appetite and may forage for food at almost any time. The tiger gecko is active almost exclusively at night and is often seen climbing up the vivarium glass and objects in the vivarium. This species and

The curled tail of this Namib giant ground gecko (*Chondrodactylus angulifer namibensis*) warns all comers that it is prepared to defend itself. This nocturnal gecko species is very active.

the viper gecko can climb easily with their adhesive pads (lamellae) under the toes, though vipers spend most of their time on the vivarium floor. Wonder geckos, the helmeted gecko, and the Namib giant ground gecko do not have adhesive lamellae under the toes and cannot climb up vivarium walls, but they will climb onto rocks and such in the vivarium to bask.

Housing

Our selected desert-dwellers are best suited to horizontally oriented vivaria. For helmeted, tiger, viper, and Namib sand geckos, glass vivaria of about 5 gallons (19 L) are suitable to house one or two specimens; a 10-gallon (38-L) tank can house up to five specimens. Slightly larger containers, 10 to 20 gallons (38 to 76 L), will suffice for one or two wonder geckos or Namib giant ground specimens. Tight-fitting lids (screen) are needed for tiger and viper geckos due to their ability to climb glass and escape from small gaps in vivarium lids that do not seal well. However, if you can find a way to safely position the basking light over the vivarium and don't have predators (such as cats) in the home, you don't really need a lid for the other species because they don't climb glass. Clear or opaque plastic storage containers can be used as vivaria; be sure to drill small (¼-inch, 6-mm) air holes in the lids and upper sides for adequate ventilation. Do not use plastic containers for tiger geckos as they may be sitting on the inside of the top when you open it and easily escape.

An incandescent basking light fashioned from a clip-on type lamp with a metal dome holder, a porcelain heat emitter, or an undertank heater will keep the vivarium warm. In colder climates, you may need both an under-tank heater and an overhead lamp to reach proper temperatures (see individual species accounts). Start with a 25-watt bulb, increasing wattage if necessary to reach the right temperature. (Household bulbs work well, but reptile bulbs may be more efficient.) If you see a desert gecko continually arching its back, it is too cold. Full-spectrum (with UV-B) reptile lighting is not necessary because these are mostly nocturnal geckos, but it won't hurt if you already have the equipment. A red or blue 25-watt incandescent bulb is great for observing your gecko at night while keeping the temperature above 65°F (18°C).

These geckos need a sandy substrate, and play sand is readily available from your local home improvement store. The depth will depend on the species being kept, but smaller geckos do well with an inch (2.5 cm) or so; larger species need 2 to 3 inches (5 to 7.5 cm). Live succulent plants (low in form and without thorns) or artificial plants give the geckos something to climb on. Other decorations can include pieces of driftwood and rocks (glued together if stacked). Do not give the geckos a "ramp" on which they can walk up to the top of the vivarium and escape. They also need at least two hiding places where they can relax— one placed in the cool end of the cage, the other in the warm end. Food and water dishes complete the decorations.

Feeding

All the desert-dwelling geckos in this chapter are meat-eaters, insectivorous to carnivorous. Feed them the most varied diet possible, including most of the following foods.

Crickets form the basis for the diet of all the species. Larger species, such as wonder geckos and sand geckos, will eat three- to five-week-old crickets about $^3/_8$ inch to $^5/_8$ inch

(10 to 16 mm) long, whereas the micro-geckos (or smaller specimens from the generally larger species) will do well on two-week-old crickets. Feed adults three or four times weekly, ten to twelve crickets per feeding. Feeding frequency may be increased in warmer weather and decreased in winter.

This Namib sand gecko (*Palmatogecko rangei*) makes a meal of a cricket. Namib sand geckos are perhaps the most available reptile from Namibia and Angola.

Large mealworms are fine for the larger wonder and sand geckos, and small mealworms can be fed to the micro-geckos. Present the mealworms in a dish that is shallow enough for the geckos, yet not so shallow that the mealworms can escape. Put calcium and vitamin supplement powder in the bottom of the dish so the mealworms will carry supplements to the geckos. Put fresh worms in every day. Many breeders use mealworms as a dietary staple. Superworms and waxworms make a great dietary supplement for larger wonder geckos and the Namib giant ground gecko. To avoid getting your geckos addicted to waxworms (geckos will often refuse other, more nutritional food after being fed waxworms on a regular basis), give them only as occasional snacks.

Larger specimens of wonder geckos and sand geckos will take an occasional pinky (a baby mouse that still has the eyes shut and is hairless) as a snack. Some breeders also feed small feeder lizards to their larger geckos.

T-Rex Leopard Gecko ICB Dust works well as a general supplement. Give powdered calcium in a separate dish for adult females to help them avoid hypocalcemia and produce more fertile eggs.

Breeding

Our selected desert-dwellers are sexually mature at an average of seven months in the male and nine months in the female. Sex is determined by presence of hemipenal bulges in the male and absence of hemipenal bulges in females. As with any gecko, females should be sufficiently robust before breeding. A temperature drop of five to ten degrees Fahrenheit (three to six degrees Celsius) from normal warm season temperatures during the winter months helps facilitate breeding in the spring.

Egg Management

Two hard-shelled eggs will be laid about thirty days after mating, usually buried into the substrate. Eggs are visible through the female's abdominal skin for several days before laying occurs. Eggs should be collected and incubated separately from the parents, as the adults may eat the hatchlings or the eggs. (Cannibalism is especially prevalent among calcium-deprived females.) A little careful digging is usually necessary to recover the fragile eggs.

To incubate the eggs, put them in a small bottle cap placed inside a larger container, such as a clear plastic 16-ounce (0.47-L) deli cup with a lid and air holes for ventilation. The eggs should be incubated at about 70 percent relative humidity. Use a hygrometer to measure humidity. The most common way to maintain this level of humidity is to use approximately 2 inches (5 cm) of moist vermiculite, perlite, or sphagnum moss placed at the bottom of the incubation container. Check the substrate periodically to make sure it is moist enough. Err on the dry side because the embryo could drown in the egg if it is too moist.

Sometimes, eggs may stick to the bottom of the vivarium or to cage decorations. Do not attempt to force stuck eggs off the surface to which they adhere; they will break with surprisingly little force. Stuck eggs should be isolated from the parents if it is not possible to collect them. Cover the eggs with a plastic medicine cup punched with air holes or with sterile medical gauze, and use tape to secure the protective cover over the eggs. In this way, the eggs can still breathe and be protected while you monitor their status. Once the babies hatch, collect them and set them up in a separate container from the adults.

Most desert gecko species may be safely incubated in the 81°F to 88°F (27°C to 31°C) temperature range. Find a place in your home or the vivarium that will stay in this range for the forty-five (small species) to seventy (larger species) days needed for incubation. As incubation temperature increases, time to hatching decreases, but very high or low temperatures will lead to developmental failures.

Hatchling Management

Hatchling desert-dwellers are simply smaller versions of their parents. They require smaller food items offered more frequently and misting the sides of the cage with water. Because they are so small, they are at risk of dehydration, but this is easy to avoid with the proper vivarium setup. To move the smallest hatchlings (the three micro-geckos as well as the Namib sand gecko), transfer them from the incubation cup by either carefully pouring them out or by encouraging them to hop onto a strip of paper towel and then moving them on the paper towel. Do not handle them as they are too fragile at this size.

For housing, use a 16-ounce (0.47-L) clear deli cup and lid with air holes. Place a few strips of paper towel inside to create a place for the gecko to sit and hide. Clutch mates can be kept together in plastic containers with a diameter of 6³/₄ inches (17 cm) and a depth of 2¹/₂ inches (6.4 cm). Place a few strips of paper towel inside to create a place for the geckos to sit and hide. Put half a toilet paper roll in the large container as a gecko shelter, and cover it with paper-towel strips. Mist the sides of the container (not the paper-towel strips) once daily so the young geckos will get a drink, and the proper humidity is maintained at the same time.

Change the towels and container frequently to keep things clean. Keep under bright fluorescent lighting and at the lower end of adult basking temperatures (about 84°F, 29°C) during the day, with nighttime temperatures in the 70°F to 75°F (21°C to 24°C) range.

Feed daily on five or six pinhead crickets to start. Miniature mealworms also work well. Supplementation is the same as for adults. When they graduate to week-old crickets, you can move them into a small glass vivarium with the same screen-top setup as for adults. The screen must be fine enough to keep the sticky-footed species from escaping. Clutch mates may be kept together in this setup as long as they don't fight and are similar in size.

The larger wonder gecko and Namib giant ground gecko hatchlings should be transferred to a new container without handling them directly. Later, move them to a small glass vivarium as described above and with the same temperature range. Small plastic critter boxes are also great for raising hatchlings. Keep the little geckos either individually or as clutch mates, but always remove larger or aggressive specimens. Feed on week-old crickets to start; but most will graduate to two-week-old crickets in two or three weeks. Hatchlings will also accept small mealworms and similar foods. Don't forget the calcium and vitamin supplements. Mist the sides of the container and the hatchlings daily.

Notes on Selected Species

The desert-dwellers are discussed roughly in order of their ease of keeping, from Geckonia as easiest to wonder geckos as most difficult.

Helmeted Gecko
Geckonia chazaliae

This species is suitable for a novice who has some gecko experience.

Helmeted geckos occur in northwestern Africa, including the countries of Senegal, Mauritania, and Morocco, where they are found in sand dunes and rocky deserts,

Though not widely available, the helmeted gecko (*Geckonia chazaliae*) is a hardy little desert gecko that adapts well to the vivarium.

though usually in moist niches. Specimens have been found living under camel dung and in trash (e.g., soda cans, boxes) on the ground.

This is a small, stout gecko with a large head vaguely resembling an armored helmet. The overall color is reddish brown with various patterns that often include a broken line of white spots down the back. Accomplished Geckonia breeder J. Stacy Yankee has produced different color and pattern morphs. This species reaches a bit over 3 inches (7.5 cm) in length. Some authorities consider the genus *Geckonia* to be a synonym of the large genus *Tarentola*.

Geckonia chazaliae has proven to be a sturdy and easy-to-breed captive. Keep it between about 79°F and 86°F (26°C and 30°C). Since helmeted geckos live in a moist coastal environment and underneath items that keep them moist, it is necessary to mist adults each time they are fed and to mist hatchlings daily.

As long as sexually mature females (four to six months of age) are adequately hydrated and are supplied with adequate calcium as part of their vitamin and mineral supplementation, they do very well as breeders and lay eggs year-round. Males are easily distinguished from females by the presence of large hemipenal bulges. Breeders have had success keeping several different combinations of helmeted geckos without conflict, including sexual pairs and trios, and even more than one male together. Incubate eggs between 84°F and 88°F (29°C and 31°C). Hatching occurs in fifty-five to sixty-five days.

Viper Gecko
Teratolepis fasciata

This species can be kept by a novice with gecko experience.

Viper geckos (*Teratolepis fasciatus*) have a distinctive color pattern and usually have a carrot-shaped tail that stores fats and water against hard times.

Viper geckos occur in Pakistan and northern India, where they inhabit arid deserts and steppes and hide under stones during the day.

This is a small gecko with a basically black and white color pattern consisting of dark, squarish blotches crossed by six rows of white spots down the back. The belly is white. The tail is inflated and carrotlike in appearance with a pattern of white scale rows on a dark brown to black background. The long, thin toes have claws and adhesive lamellae. Few specimens exceed 4 inches (10 cm) in length.

This docile little gecko is very easy to manage in the vivarium. Maintain the cage temperature between 90°F and 95°F (32°C and 35°C) at the warmest end of the vivarium. Mist directly when feeding. This micro-gecko is a prolific breeder and can be kept in sexual pairs, trios, or a combination of one male and up to five females in a suitable vivarium; 10 gallons (38 L) or larger is easiest to manage because high temperatures are needed. (It is more difficult to establish a thermal gradient in a smaller setup.) Do not keep sexually mature males together! Incubation should be at 88°F to 90°F (31°C to 32°C) at about 80 percent relative humidity. The eggs will hatch in about forty-five days.

Tiger or Thick-Toed Gecko
Pachydactylus tigrinus

This species is for the novice keeper with gecko experience.

There are many African species in the genus *Pachydactylus*; the most familiar and colorful is the tiger gecko (*Pachydactylus tigrinus*). Few are found in the vivarium, however, as this species does not tolerate humid climates well.

The genus *Pachydactylus* (the thick-toed geckos) is a large group native to southern Africa. The only species frequently seen in the vivarium, however, is *Pachydactylus tigrinus*, which occurs in southeastern Africa in Zimbabwe, the Republic of South Africa, eastern Botswana, and western Mozambique. There it is found in arid habitats, where it sleeps under objects during the day and emerges at night to feed and to mate.

This small gecko has reddish to brownish background coloration with black spotting and fine, raised white spots in wavy rows from the neck to the tail. There is a black lateral stripe running from the nose to the ear. The tail stores fat and regenerates if lost. Adhesive lamellae under the toes allow this gecko to climb vertical surfaces. Adults are about 3$\frac{1}{2}$ inches (9 cm) long.

The tiger gecko is hardy, but it is nervous and prefers not to be handled. Maintain the cage temperature between 86°F and 88°F (30°C and 31°C) during the day. Mist only a corner of the vivarium when feeding, as this species does not tolerate humidity very well, especially when they are hatchlings. The recommended breeding situation is either sexual pairs or one male with multiple females. Females are prolific breeders and will lay eggs year-round. Eggs are usually laid under objects, such as hide boxes. Adults do not seem to bother the hatchlings if the eggs are allowed to hatch out in the vivarium, but immediate removal of hatchlings is recommended because a hungry adult might find the young inviting as a meal. I have noted that hatchlings from eggs allowed to incubate in the vivarium at the above temperatures are predominantly female. Incubation in the middle to upper eighties Farenheit (29°C to 31°C) results in hatching in about forty-five days. Incubation may take longer if temperatures are on the cool side. Raise hatchlings individually as one clutch mate will usually be dominant when feeding.

Namib Giant Ground Gecko
Chondrodactylus angulifer

This species (also known as the giant Namibian sand gecko) is recommended for the intermediate keeper who has some gecko experience.

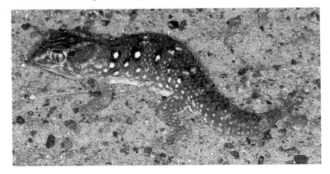

The large white spots of the male Namib giant ground gecko (*Chondrodactylus angulifer angulifer*) give it a distinctive appearance. Quite aggressive, this gecko is not afraid to bite and should be handled carefully if at all.

Chondrodactylus angulifer has two subspecies, *C. angulifer angulifer* and *C. angulifer namibensis*, that occur in the Republic of South Africa, Namibia, and Botswana. They are found in arid to semiarid deserts and sleep under objects on the ground during the day. *C. a. angulifer* has a slightly stockier build than *C. a. namibensis* and is sexually dimorphic in that males have large white spots in paired rows on either side of the body. *C. a. namibensis* lacks this sexual dimorphism; in both sexes, white tubercles are present on the back. In *C. a. angulifer* the belly scales get bigger going up the gecko's sides, but in *C. a. namibensis* the belly scales get smaller going up the gecko's sides. Both of these subspecies have much variation in color, from bright to dull reddish browns. Adults may be 6 inches (15 cm) long.

Giant ground geckos are hardy captives best suited for experienced gecko keepers, mainly due to their quick and sometimes unpredictable aggressive behavior when the keeper's hands are in the vivarium. These geckos have massive jaws and are capable of inflicting a painful bite! This aggressiveness is a display of their natural instinct to always be on the alert for food items. (If you see *Chondrodactylus angulifer* arch their tails up like a scorpion, they are in defensive mode.) Their frequent patrols for food make them observable during part of the day as well as most of the night.

Chondrodactylus angulifer can be kept in sexual pairs or other combinations of one male (do not keep males together) and several females, adjusting vivarium size for more individuals. A 20-gallon (76-L) vivarium can house a male and two females. These geckos like to burrow, so give them something to burrow into. Even a simple vivarium setup with 2 to 3 inches (5 to 7.5 cm) of sand substrate will do. Paper-towel rolls are the perfect size for hiding places, so put at least one roll per gecko in the vivarium. Cork-bark tubes and other shelters may be used as long as they are sturdy and allow the gecko to hide completely. During the day, maintain the warm end of the vivarium between 88°F and 95°F (31°C and 35°C) and mist the cool side of the vivarium daily in addition to using a water dish.

Females will bury their eggs, so if you see sand piled up in the vivarium, you know there is a good chance eggs have been laid. Eggs are somewhat fragile, so take care in removing them. Do not attempt to remove eggs that are stuck to the floor or sides of the vivarium or to any cage decorations. Cover them with a cup or sterile gauze as previously mentioned. Giant ground geckos exhibit temperature-dependent sex determination; eggs incubated at about 70 percent relative humidity and at 80°F (27°C) yield mostly female offspring in about sixty days. As incubation temperatures are increased, the ratio will skew to a higher number of male hatchlings. The young are precocious and should be raised individually due to size differentials that usually develop from competition for food.

The many small white spots on the back show this to be the subspecies *Chondrodactylus angulifer namibensis* of the Namib giant ground gecko.

Hatchlings display a banded pattern; as the lizards grow, the bands break up until eventually the adult pattern is attained. *Chondrodactylus a. angulifer* young are easily sexed at hatching, as males display prominent white spots while females are marked with white bands.

Namib Sand or Web-Footed Gecko
Palmatogecko rangei

This species is recommended for the intermediate keeper with gecko experience.

Palmatogecko rangei occurs in the western Republic of South Africa, Namibia, and southern Angola. There it occurs in virtually barren sand dunes, spending the daytime in relatively moist tunnels.

This odd gecko is a small, slender species known for its webbed feet and the transparency of its skin. Its color ranges from pink to brown with a variable degree of mottled black patterns on the back. A faint white stripe runs down the back and tail, allowing the gecko's spine to be visible through the skin. The creamy white of the belly extends about half-way up the gecko's flanks. The tail regenerates if lost. *Palmatogecko rangei* can reach about 5 inches (12.7 cm) long.

The Namib sand gecko has proven to be an interesting and hardy captive species with a very docile demeanor. A simple, functional enclosure is a plastic shoebox with a lid. Drill two ¼-inch (6-mm) holes on each side of the container about 1 inch (2.5 cm) from the top. Put about a ½

In the Namib sand gecko (*Palmatogecko rangei*), the toes are fully webbed, allowing these little geckos to quickly scamper over loose sand at night. Males (top) tend to be more weakly banded than females (bottom).

inch (12.7 mm) of sand on the bottom, add a hide box in both the cool and warm ends, and give the gecko some low dishes for food and water. Maintain the enclosure between 84°F and 90°F (29°C and 32°C) in the warmest part of the vivarium during the day. UTHs work well with plastic shoe-boxes to achieve the proper temperature. This gecko has been observed active at very low temperatures in nature, as low as 30°F (-1°C) (Bruce Gates, pers. comm.), so a night-time temperature drop to as low as 50°F (10°C) will be tolerated easily. Hydration is critical to success with the Namib sand gecko—this species has been observed standing in thick fogs, licking the moisture that develops on their jaws and face. Spray the gecko directly with a fine mist of tepid water at each feeding, and mist one corner of the vivarium nightly on a surface the gecko can lick.

The tiny size of this Namib sand gecko hatchling is clearly illustrated by its ability to fit easily on a quarter.

Breeding pairs and trios live compatibly, and even multiple males are known to get along in breeding situations, provided vivarium setups are large enough to accommodate them. A 16-quart (15.2-L) plastic storage container or 10-gallon (38-L) glass vivarium will work well. Females lay their eggs under shelters and landscaping in the vivarium. Eggshells of this species are thin, so take extra care when removing them for incubation. Incubating at 80°F (27°C) results in hatchlings appearing in about sixty to sixty-five days.

Wonder Geckos
Genus Teratoscincus
The wonder geckos are species for the intermediate keeper with some gecko experience.

Two species of wonder geckos (there are several others in the genus) are fairly easy to find for the vivarium. The wonder gecko, *Teratoscincus scincus*, and the frog-eyed wonder gecko also called Roborowski's gecko, *T. roborowski*, are part of a small group of strange geckos from arid steppes and desert regions of Central Asia (including western China), parts of the former Soviet Union, and ranging west to the Arabian Peninsula. *T. scincus* is found in virtually this entire area, but *T. roborowski* is thought to occur only in the Turpan Depression, Turpan Prefecture, Xinjiang Province, and Gansu Province, northwestern China. Both species live in sand dunes and moist, deep burrows in the desert.

Both species of *Teratoscincus* discussed here are covered with dark bands that become more flecked with cream as the gecko ages. In *T. scincus*, the bands are brown, and in *T. roborowski* the bands are a brownish orange. The body is covered in fishlike or skinklike scales that can be dislodged easily by handling, which necessitates indirect handling techniques such as moving them in a cup or net. *T. scincus* ranges from 5 to 8 inches (12 to 20 cm) long, and *T. roborowski* grows to about 5 inches (12.7 cm) long.

If you hear *Teratoscincus* geckos rattle their scales, they are exhibiting courtship or territorial or defense behavior.

All the species of the genus *Teratoscincus* are called wonder geckos or frog-eyed geckos, which means that it is important to know the correct scientific name when discussing species of this genus. This frog-eyed gecko is Roborowski's gecko, *Teratoscincus roborowski*.

For this they use enlarged scales that run down the upper surface of the tail and are rubbed against each other.

Teratoscincus geckos are nocturnal, terrestrial, burrowing geckos. It is possible to set up a simulated burrowing situation for them in captivity if you wish. To do this, use at least a 15- to 20-gallon (57- to 76-L) glass vivarium for a pair of these active geckos. Be sure to put the cage in its permanent location before putting the sand in or it will be too heavy to move! Pour about 6 inches (15 cm) of sand in the bottom of the vivarium. Designate one end as the moist side; spray the sand with water and mix it in. Cover an $8^{1}/_{2} \times 6 \times 3$-inch (21 $\times$ 15 $\times$ 7.5-cm) commercial plastic hide box or similar PVC pipe with sand on the moist end to provide an entrance to the burrow. Insert a smaller diameter PVC pipe vertically into the moist side, and put water in it daily to keep the moisture level up in the burrow. Spray one side of the vivarium in the evening to provide a drink of water for your pet. The next step in setting up your *Teratoscincus* vivarium is to use a clamp-light with an incandescent bulb housed in a metal dome. Start with a 25-watt bulb and increase wattage as needed to maintain a surface temperature of 95°F to 100°F (35°C to 38°C) during the day. Nighttime temperatures can range between 68°F and 72°F (20°C and 22°C). In the winter, *Teratoscincus* geckos are accustomed to hibernate, so gradually lower temperatures to 50°F to 60°F (10°C to 16°C) for a three-month period. In the spring, gradually warm the geckos. A temperature drop in the winter is necessary if you wish your geckos to breed in the spring. Sexual pairs work well in breeding these geckos. The two eggs hatch in roughly fifty to sixty days when incubated at temperatures between 77°F and 90°F (25°C and 32°C).

REFERENCES

Bragg, W. K., J. D. Fawcett, T. B. Bragg, and B. E. Viets. 2000. Nest-site selection in two eublepharid gecko species with temperature-dependent sex and one with genotypic sex determination. *Zoological Journal of the Linnean Society* 69: 319–332.

Christenson, G., and L. Christenson. 2003. *Day Geckos in Captivity.* Ada, Okla.: Living Art Publishing.

de Vosjoli, P., F. Fast, and A. Repashy. 2003. *Rhacodactylus: The Complete Guide to Their Selection and Care.* Vista, Calif.: Advanced Visions.

de Vosjoli, P., R. Tremper, and R. Klingenberg. 2005. *Herpetoculture of Leopard Geckos: Twenty-Seven Generations of Living Art.* Vista, Calif.: Advanced Visions.

Svatek, S., and S. van Duin. 2001. *Leaf-Tailed Geckos: The Genus Uroplatus.* Banteln, Germany: Brahmer Verlag.

Viets, B. E., M. A. Ewert, L. G. Talent, and C. E. Nelson. 1994. "Sex-Determining Mechanisms in Squamate Reptiles." *Journal of Experimental Zoology* 270: 45–56.

RECOMMENDED READING

In addition to the books and articles noted in the reference section, the following printed and online resources will prove helpful in your continued study of geckos.

Books

de Vosjoli, P. *Crested Geckos*. Irvine, Calif.: Advanced Vivarium Systems, 2005.

de Vosjoli, P., R. Klingenberg, R. Tremper, and B. Viets. *The Leopard Gecko Manual*. Irvine, Calif.: Advanced Vivarium Systems, 2004.

McKeown, S. and J. Zaworski. *General Care and Maintenance of Tokay Geckos*. Irvine, Calif.: Advanced Vivarium Systems, 1997.

Periodical Articles

Girard, F. "Captive Husbandry and Reproduction of *Teratoscinus Scincus*." *Dactylus*, 1996, 3 (1): 4–6.

Knight, M. C. "Tail Stridulation Behavior in *Teratoscincus Scincus*." *Dactylus*, 1992, 3 (1): 4–6.

Lui, W. "In Search of Roborowski's Gecko, *Teratoscincus Roborowski*." *Dactylus*, 1994, 2 (3): 93–97.

Web Sites

Association of Reptilian and Amphibian Veterinarians
http://www.arav.org/
Useful for finding a reptile veterinarian in your area. This site also has information on salmonellosis.

Center for Disease Control and Prevention
http://www.cdc.gov/healthypets/animals/reptiles.htm
Find information on zoonoses, diseases that are transmittable from animals to humans.

Family Gekkonidae
http://www.embl-heidelberg.de/~uetz/families/
Gekkonidae.html
This site, maintained by J. Boone and B. Klusmeyer, contains an updated listing of described reptiles, including the genera and species of Gekkonidae and Eublepharidae.

Global Gecko Association
http://www.gekkota.com/
A society dedicated to gecko enthusiasts worldwide. Membership is open to anyone with an interest in gekkonids, from the professional herpetologist to the hobbyist. Publishes the newsletter *Chit-Chat* and the journal *Gekko*.

Herp Vet Connection
http://www.herpvetconnection.com/
At this site, you can get recommendations from clients of veterinarians in your area.

Kingsnake.com
http://www.kingsnake.com/
Commercial Web site with many vendors and links.

Reptiles Magazine
http://www.reptilesmagazine.com/
A monthly publication covering herps from *A* to *Z*. The Web site provides useful care tips as well as links to breeders, photo galleries, and message boards.

Uroplatus.com
http://www.uroplatus.com/
This is an international Web site for all gecko enthusiasts.

INDEX

New Caledonian geckos
(*Rhacodactylus*): about
genus, 11, 12, 119–20; feeding, 123–24; housing,
120–23; reproduction,
124–26
New Zealand gecko (*Naultinus*),
17
nocturnal geckos, 10–11
Nosy Be leaf-tailed gecko
(*Uroplatus ebenaui*),
100–101. *See also* leaf-tailed
geckos
novice gecko keepers, 23–24

O
orchid bark substrate, 31
outdoor vivaria, 121
overcrowding, 45

P
parasites, 48–49, 96
Paroedura. See Madagascan
ground geckos
patterns and colors, 15–16, 57,
63, 64–65, 110
peacock day gecko (*Phelsuma
quadriocellata quadrio-
cellata*), 39, 89–91. *See also*
day geckos
Phelsuma. See day geckos
pheromones for marking territory, 19
photoperiod, 37, 58
pinky mice, 60
plants for vivarium, 32
PVC pipe, 32

Q
quarantine, 45–47

R
reading list, 152–53
reef gecko (*Sphaerodactylus*), 12
reproduction, 17. *See also*
breeding, egg, and hatchling
management
resources for more information,
152–53
respiratory infections, 54

Rhacodactylus. See New
Caledonian geckos
Roborowski's gecko
(*Teratoscincus roborowski*),
134. *See also* desert geckos
rubber jaw, 52

S
salmonellosis, 47–48
sand substrates, 30
satanic leaf-tailed gecko
(*Uroplatus phantasticus*), 15,
25, 93, 101–2. *See also* leaf-
tailed geckos
scales and skin, 16
scientific names, proper care
based on, 26–27
self-fertilization, 17
sexing, 19
sexual maturity, food amounts
and, 41
shedding, 16–17, 50, 51
shopping: for gecko foods, 39;
for geckos, 26, 42–43
sick versus healthy geckos, feces
of, 46. *See also* veterinarians
skin: scales and, 16; shedding,
16–17, 50, 51; signs of
healthy gecko, 26
skunk gecko (*Gekko vittatus*), 9,
10–11, 111–15, 117–18
small Madagascan ground gecko
(*Paroedura androyensis*),
108–9. *See also* Madagascan
ground geckos
spear-point leaf-tailed gecko
(*Uroplatus ebenaui*), 100–101.
See also leaf-tailed geckos
species, mixing (not), 44–45
spectacle or brille (eye covering),
14
sphagnum moss substrate, 31
Standing's day gecko (*Phelsuma
standingi*), 24, 74, 79, 91–92.
See also day geckos
stress: coloration indicators, 21,
46, 95; sources of, 44–45
substrates, 30–31; gut impaction
from, 30, 51; and shed
problems, 50

ABOUT THE EDITOR

Julie Bergman is a recognized reptile breeder who has been raising geckos for more than twenty-two years. In 1993, Bergman founded Gecko Ranch, a company catering to gecko owners and enthusiasts. Gecko Ranch geckos are award winning and have been selected for show by prestigious zoological facilities, including the San Antonio Zoo and Aquarium, the Fort Worth Zoo, San Francisco's Conservatory of Flowers, and the Living Desert Zoo in Palm Desert, California. Her company has been featured on television programs such as *Good Day Sacramento*, KCRA Channel 3 News, and *California Heartland* on PBS. Bergman earned a bachelor's degree in biological psychology from the University of California–Davis and has spoken at numerous herpetological societies. She is a freelance writer for *Reptiles* magazine and a member of Psi Chi National Honor Society, the Global Gecko Association, the Pet Industry Joint Advisory Council, and the Northern California Herpetological Society. You can contact Bergman through her Web site at http//www.geckoranch.com.